A Practical Guide to

Social Impact Assessment

For the real world

By Andrea Kanaris

First published by Ultimate World Publishing 2025
Copyright © 2025 Andrea Kanaris

ISBN

Paperback: 978-1-923425-25-5
Ebook: 978-1-923425-26-2

Andrea Kanaris has asserted her rights under the Copyright, Designs and Patents Act 1988 to be identified as the author of this work. The information in this book is based on the author's experiences and opinions. The publisher specifically disclaims responsibility for any adverse consequences which may result from use of the information contained herein. Permission to use information has been sought by the author. Any breaches will be rectified in further editions of the book.

All rights reserved. No part of this publication may be reproduced, stored in or introduced into a retrieval system, or transmitted in any form, or by any means (electronic, mechanical, photocopying, recording or otherwise) without the prior written permission of the author. Any person who does any unauthorised act in relation to this publication may be liable to criminal prosecution and civil claims for damages. Enquiries should be made through the publisher.

Cover design: Ultimate World Publishing
Layout and typesetting: Ultimate World Publishing
Editor: Vanessa McKay
Cover Image Copyright: Rawpixel.com-Shutterstock.com

Ultimate World Publishing
Diamond Creek,
Victoria Australia 3089
www.writeabook.com.au

1 Testimonials

"Andrea is a highly intelligent, effective practitioner with wide ranging experience. She worked on several projects with me at ImpaxSIA and always delivered work of a high quality on time."

Dr Annie Holden

"Good projects deliver positive legacy outcomes for communities and manage the negative impacts that arise during development, operations and decommissioning. Andrea draws on her extensive experience in Australia and internationally to provide social impact professionals with a practical tool to help them apply theoretical frameworks and best practice in meaningful ways to deliver locally specific, positive change. This includes guidance on how to unlock project resources and commitment to ensure assessments are more than just ticking a box for compliance."

Louisa Cass, Acclimate Partners

"Andrea is safe hands. She is a highly competent social practitioner who produces valuable insights as a researcher and strategic advisor. She has a deep understanding of social impact assessment and management, and adapts her processes to cater to clients' particular needs and priorities without compromising quality. "

Paul McLeod, Founder | Managing Director, Risk Communications Australia

"Social impact assessment is a highly complex and ever-evolving field of practice. It is also poorly understood beyond the field itself, often being conflated with community engagement, and often confined to desktop studies that exclude affected communities. Applying and integrating multiple social science disciplines, SIA seeks to understand and evaluate how environmental change affects people and communities, and to support better social and cultural outcomes over time, with a focus on equity, fairness, and justice. With careful and ethical application of multiple social research methods, people affected by development can use their local knowledge to shape project design and determine their own futures.

This complexity demands that people embarking on this practice – whether they be practitioners, researchers, regulators, or project-affected communities – have access to insightful, reflexive, and practical advice and guidance. Andrea Kanaris has been at the forefront of SIA practice for many years, and now shares her extensive experience in this book."

Dr Richard Parsons, CENVP (SIA)

"Andrea's book is a testament to her expertise and experience in the field. Having worked with Andrea in the past, I can vouch for her depth of knowledge in social impact assessment and management.

She is thorough in her reviews and provides critical analysis and solutions, supporting navigating the complexities of the social impact assessment and management process.

Working with Andrea is an absolute pleasure. Her approachable nature and willingness to share her knowledge makes working with her enjoyable and a learning experience.

I look forward to reading and using Andrea's book, "A Practical Guide for Social Impact Assessment".

Carla Martinez, Social Performance National Executive, WSP Australia

It was a real privilege to work alongside Andrea Kanaris in the development of the Queensland Office of the Coordinator-General's Social Impact Assessment Guideline. Andrea's deep expertise in social science methodologies, coupled with her practical approach to impact assessment, played a pivotal role in shaping a robust and practical guideline that has since set a high standard for social impact assessments in Queensland.

Andrea brought a wealth of experience to the project, drawing on over 30 social impact assessments across Australia and internationally. Her ability to bridge the gap between regulatory requirements and real-world community engagement was instrumental in crafting a guideline that is both technically rigorous and practically applicable. Not only does the guideline reflect international best practice, it is tailored to the unique regulatory landscape of Queensland.

Andrea strongly advocates for community-focused impact assessments. She champions the importance of meaningful stakeholder engagement, the application of ethical research methodologies, and the integration of social performance into project planning from the outset.

'A Practical Guide to Social Impact Assessment in The Real World' is a timely contribution to the development of SIA practice and will greatly assist regulatory pathways.

Adam Caddies, Office of Coordinator General, Queensland Government

Contents

1 Testimonials iii
About the Author 1
Acknowledgements 3
Introduction 5
2 Foundations of Social Impact Assessment 11
    2.1 Principles of SIA 11
    2.2 Precautionary Principle 12
    2.3 Avoid and minimise hierarchy 13
    2.4 Free prior informed consent 13
    2.5 Defining Social Impacts 14
    2.6 Role of social impact practitioner 17
    2.7 Other roles in delivery of SIA 18
    2.8 Evidence base for determining and assessing social impacts 19
        2.8.1 Primary data sources 20
        2.8.2 Secondary data sources 20
    2.9 Community and Stakeholder Engagement in SIA 20
3 Costing a Social Impact Assessment 23
    3.1 Request for Proposal 23
        3.1.1 Step 1: Determine the regulatory requirements and standards for the SIA 26
        3.1.2 Step 2 Identify potentially affected communities 27
        3.1.3 Step 3 Determine the SIA study area 32

3.1.4 Step 4 identify potential vulnerable groups and locations 34

3.1.5 Step 5 Determine an appropriate detailed methodology 36

3.1.6 Step 6 Identify resources for delivery of the SIA 47

3.1.7 Step 7 Propose a timeline for delivery 49

3.1.8 Step 8 Costing 52

    3.1.8.1 Inclusions and exclusions 56

    3.1.8.2 Deliverables and timeframe 57

3.1.9 Step 9 Demonstrate your capability and capacity to deliver the SIA 57

3.1.10 Step 10 Write your Response to RFP 58

4 Conducting a Social impact Assessment 61

4.1 Phase 1 Scoping and initiation 61

4.2 Phase 2 SIA delivery 63

4.2.1 Stage 1 Social Baseline 63

    4.2.1.1 SIA Study area and social area of influence 66

    4.2.1.2 Vulnerable groups and social infrastructure ... 68

    4.2.1.3 Directly and indirectly impacted 72

    4.2.1.4 Retrieving data 72

    4.2.1.5 Data management 75

4.2.2 Stage 2 Field Study 77

    4.2.2.1 Preparing for field study 78

4.2.3 Stage 3 Data Analysis and Review 82

    4.2.3.1 Qualitative data 82

    4.2.3.2 Quantitative data 83

    4.2.3.3 Triangulation 83

Contents

    4.2.4 Stage 4 Social Impact Identification........................... 86
    4.2.5 Stage 5 Social Impact and Benefit Assessment 87
        4.2.5.1 Step 1 Prepare for the assessment 88
        4.2.5.2 Step 2 Conduct the social risk workshop 92
    4.2.6 Stage 6 Social Impact Management Plan 97
        4.2.6.1 Mitigation and Enhancement Strategies 98
        4.2.6.2 Monitoring and Evaluation 99
    4.2.7 Stage 7 Cumulative Impacts..101
        4.2.7.1 Step 1 Determine cumulative impacts 102
        4.2.7.2 Step 2 Assess cumulative effects........................ 103
    4.2.8 Stage 8 Reporting.. 104
        4.2.8.1 Standalone SIA Report 104
        4.2.8.2 Social Chapter..106
    4.2.9 Stage 9 Submissions 107

5 List of Resources and Regulation.................................*109*
6 Acronyms..*113*
7 References..*115*

About the Author

Andrea Kanaris is a social scientist and social impact professional, coach, mentor and Director of All Things Social Impact, helping individuals and organisations develop the skills and knowledge needed to achieve positive social change through practical processes and applications. She gained a Bachelor of Social Science – Community and International Development and Masters (Post Graduate Diploma) in Social Planning and Development from the University of Queensland.

Andrea has over 20 years' experience and is committed to the application of social science methods in the assessment of social impacts. Andrea has led over 40 social impact assessments (SIA) of renewable, infrastructure and resource projects across Australia, Indonesia and UK. She has an in-depth understanding of the requirements and expectations of regulators. She authored the Queensland Office of the Coordinator General's (OCG) Social Impact Assessment Guideline, March 2018. Her previous experience in Public Health in Queensland and UK had her conduct large scale social and health impact assessments of the South East Queensland Regional Plan and South Yorkshire Local Transport Plan (UK). This experience is reflected in her integration of health impacts into her SIA methodology. Andrea is well versed in environmental impact statement (EIS) processes and works to ensure that potential project social impacts are identified, articulated, and ultimately understood and considered by decision-makers.

Acknowledgements

This book would not exist if it were not for the long list of mentors, most significant being Associate Professor David Ip, may he rest in peace, who not only introduced me to social impact assessment but inspired, mentored and coached me.

Dr Annie Holden, you have worn many hats throughout the years, boss, business partner, mentor and friend. I thank you for your generosity in taking the time to provide invaluable insights, guidance, and encouragement. To colleagues and clients who provided recommendations, I appreciate you and your support.

To my dear friends, Rachel Richardson, Kent Buddle, and Andrea Casasola for taking the time to provide insights that made sure this book was accessible to a broad audience. Most of all I am grateful for your support and encouragement.

Introduction

Dear Reader,

Congratulations on your purchase and the pursuit of your social impact journey. I am honoured to be part of your learning and growth.

After over 20 years of applying university social science education across a range of industries and settings, being involved in over forty social impact assessments (SIA) and having guided and mentored many young budding social impact professionals, I identified a gap. This book is designed to fill the void and focusses on social impact assessment for regulatory approval in Australia. A link to regulatory frameworks in other jurisdictions can be found at the back of this book.

If you fit one of the below descriptions, this book is for you:

- Graduate or soon to be graduate of a social science (e.g., sociology, human geography, anthropology, social or community planning (State of New South Wales, 2023a)) seeking a career in social impact assessment.

- Working for an engineering firm or environmental consultancy and are involved in preparing social impact assessments as part of an environmental approvals process.

- Government regulator responsible for conducting adequacy assessment of social impact assessments.

- Proponent of a project that is seeking regulatory approval and needs to engage a social impact professional to conduct a social impact assessment.

- Proponent seeking a social impact professional to either develop, implement, and/or review your social impact management plan.

Regulators have discovered, after reviewing many social impact assessments, inconsistency in standards e.g., reporting wasn't robust, not rigorous enough, not conducted by someone with skills, research or proper methodologies. Many social impact assessments historically were not delivered by a social scientist and often resemble a tick the box exercise to meet certification, not about identifying or exploring social impact or management.

To address this problem, Queensland and New South Wales (NSW) took actions to rectify the problem and lift the standard of social impact assessment in the mining and resourcing sectors.

- Queensland developed the Strong and Sustainable Resource Communities Act (2017) (SSRC Act) following the 2015 inquiry into fly-in fly-out (FIFO) workforces, a strategy adopted to moderate the boom-bust cycle experienced in mining towns when employees reside locally. The social impact assessment guideline released in 2018 is a statutory instrument of the SSRC Act for large resource projects and a guidance for other projects.

- ❖ New South Wales developed a comprehensive, and prescriptive, social impact assessment guideline, technical supplement and scoping worksheet for the state's significant mining, petroleum production and extractive industry in 2017. The guideline outlines the need for social science methods and adequate qualifications for preparing a social impact assessment. In 2020, the guideline was revised and expanded for use in all state significant development, state significant infrastructure and critical state significant infrastructure projects.

The changing environment has not been limited to Australia, and we are seeing a global shift that has seen increasing focus on the 'Social' in environmental, social and governance reporting requirements. This emphasis on social sustainability and reporting, not only on internal practices, but on social performance regarding community outcomes and impact, has seen social impact becoming more mainstream.

Over time we have seen an increase in protests on large scale projects, particularly in mining. Protestors of the Adani project in Queensland attracted huge media attention. While in New South Wales, the Rocky Hill decision was the first time a project was rejected and stopped because of social impacts. The power of protestors, social media, the climate change agenda and aspirations of the younger generation wanting to make an impact has influenced the regulatory landscape.

This brings us back to the gap. In the process of developing social assessment and performance teams and mentoring young and emerging social impact professionals I noticed that they all were extremely bright and well educated in social science theory. Yet, they all repeatedly asked the same question: "How do I do it?". This highlights the difference between theory and practice. Both are essential and in the social impact profession there is no shortage of high-quality research and information on social impact assessment. I have included a list of resources in the back of this book that I use regularly. That aside, there is a shortage of practical and pragmatic guidance on the application of these theories in the real world. This book steps you through a real-world social impact assessment.

To use this book, you can follow the road map (Figure 1), from receiving a request to provide a fee proposal, scoping, delivery through to responding to submissions. You can follow the process from beginning to end or you can choose any step in the process where you need practical guidance. The book assumes you have a degree of theoretical underpinning knowledge and provides tips (yellow box), things for you to consider (blue box), and examples (orange box). I have provided links to well established and reputable guidance and information designed to elevate the rigour of your social impact assessment.

I am inspired by the next generation of social impact professionals, and I offer my experience in the practical application of social science methods in social impact assessment in this book to guide you on your journey to achieve your career aspirations.

Introduction

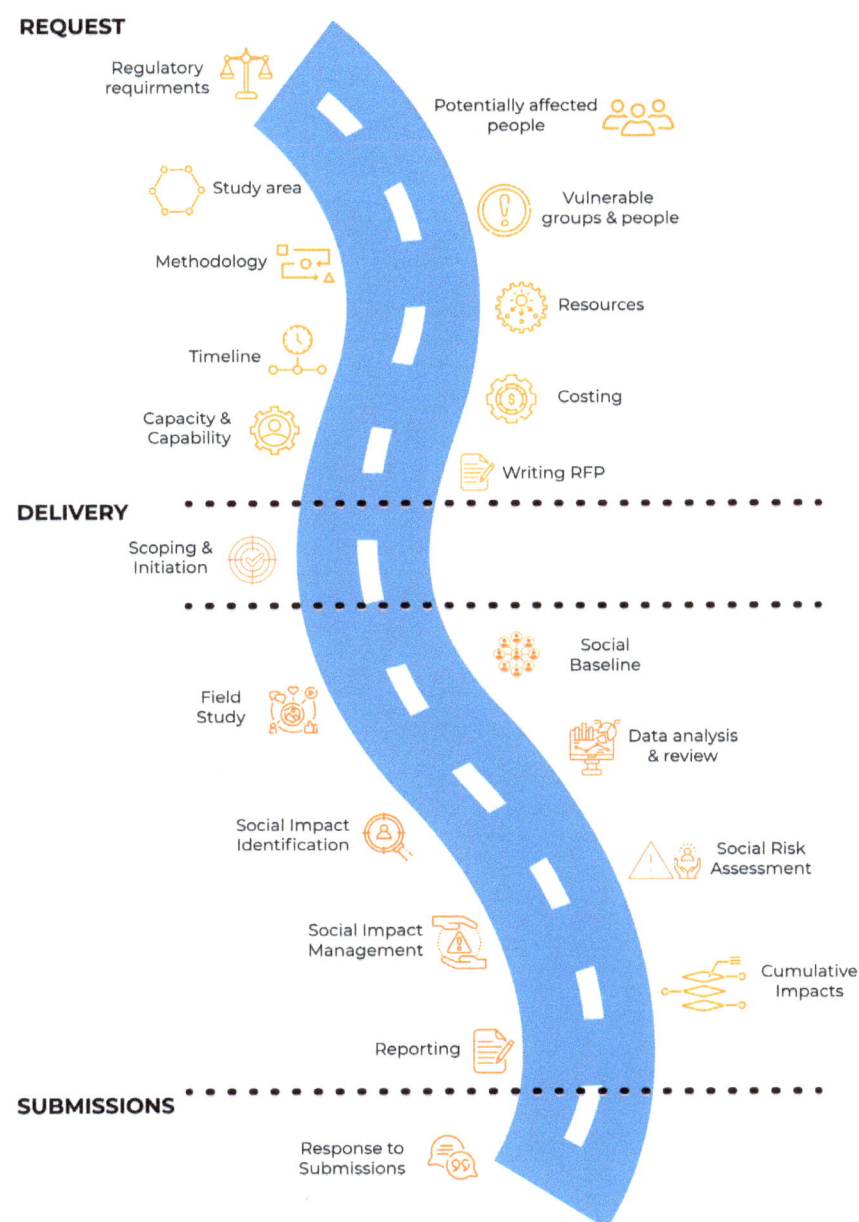

Figure 1 SIA road map

2 Foundations of Social Impact Assessment

Before we dive into the practice of social impact assessment, we should consider some of the foundations that will guide your SIA and ensure it remains consistent and aligned with international good practice.

Apply the principles that are relevant to the SIA. Consider the scope and scale of the project or intervention being assessed. Remember to articulate the rationale when not adhering to principles.

2.1 Principles of SIA

Below are principles that will support an evidence-based SIA:

Action-oriented
Defines specific actions to deliver practical, achievable and effective outcomes for people.

Adaptive
Establishes systems to respond to new or different circumstances to support continuous improvement.

Culturally responsive
Develops culturally informed approaches and methodologies to ensure Aboriginal and culturally diverse communities are engaged appropriately, and their perspectives, insights and feedback are valued.

Distributive equity
Considers how different groups will experience social impacts divergently (particularly vulnerable and marginalised groups, future generations compared with current generations, and differences by gender, age and cultural group).

Impartial
Uses fair, unbiased research methods and follows relevant ethical standards.

Inclusive
Seeks to hear, understand, respect and document the perspectives of all likely affected people. Uses respectful, meaningful and effective engagement activities tailored to the needs of those being engaged (e.g., being culturally sensitive and accessible).

Integrated
Uses and references relevant information and analysis from other assessments to avoid duplication. Supports effective interaction of social, economic and environmental considerations in decision-making.

Life-cycle focus
Seeks to understand likely impacts (including cumulative impacts) at all project stages, from pre-construction to post-closure/operation commencement.

Material
Identify which likely social impacts matter the most to people and/or pose the greatest risk/opportunity to those expected to be affected.

Source: (State of New South Wales, 2023) (Vanclay, 2003; Vanclay et al., 2015)

When applying the principles, it is important to note that SIA is not a top-down process. It provides an opportunity to inform design based on community input, build capacity, resilience and social capital.

2.2 Precautionary Principle

The precautionary principle requires consideration of:

1. Careful evaluation to avoid, wherever practicable, serious or irreversible damage to the communities, and

2. An assessment of the risk weighted consequences of various options (Australian Government, 1992).

2.3 Avoid and minimise hierarchy

The avoid and minimise hierarchy requires that the SIA considers:

1. Avoiding impacts to the community as much as possible. This can include screening potential risks and selecting a different development site.

2. If avoidance isn't possible, minimise the impact by using more community friendly methods. For example, you can limit the hours of a construction project to avoid disturbance to nearby residents (Government – Office of the Coordinator-General, 2018).

2.4 Free prior informed consent

Free, prior, and informed consent (FPIC) is a process for ensuring that all peoples are provided the right to self-determination (Food and Agriculture Organisation, 2016). Key elements include:

- Voluntary consent, free from coercion, intimidation or manipulation.

- Consent is sought prior to authorisation or commencement of activities, during early stages of development and investment plans, and not only when approval from the community is required.

❖ People are informed as part of seeking consent and is ongoing throughout the process. The engagement should be transparent, accessible, clear, consistent, and accurate (Food and Agriculture Organisation, 2016).

FPIC is important because it respects Indigenous Peoples' rights to self-determination and cultural development, involves people in decisions that affect them, and actively seeks to avoid force or threat to obtain consent from Indigenous Peoples (Food and Agriculture Organisation, 2016).

Australia has not passed legislation on FPIC (Corrs Chambers Westgarth, 2023). The issue is addressed under the Native Title Act 1993, which emphasises the importance of Traditional Owners' knowledge of the land (Australian Institute of Aboriginal and Torres Strait Islander Studies, n.d.).

You can get more detailed guidance from the FPIC Manual for practitioners:

https://openknowledge.fao.org

2.5 Defining Social Impacts

Using consistent language for how you define social impacts is important. It will allow you to differentiate social impacts from other impacts identified in technical studies such as air quality, noise, traffic, water, visual, flood, etc. Given social impact assessment is predictive in nature, it is best to think in terms of potential social impacts which can be:

- Positive social impact refers to the beneficial effects a project, policy or program has on people and society, including improvements like increased access to education, better health outcomes, promoting equality, supporting the local economy (Sopact, n.d.), and generally enhancing the well-being of a community (Mizrak, 2023).

- Negative social impact refers to harmful effects of project, policy or program on a community's well-being, including things like increased inequality, displacement of people, environmental degradation, crime rates, cultural erosion, social exclusion, and economic decline (Sopact, n.d.).

- Cumulative social impact refers to the combined, gradually accumulating negative effects on a community or society that result from multiple, often seemingly small, social stressors occurring over time, where the combined impact becomes significantly detrimental to the well-being of the people affected (United States Environmental Protection Agency, 2025). It may also be an accumulation of negative effects of multiple development projects that overlap in the same region.

Table 1 defines the social impact categories and associated definition in relation to the consequence or change that may be experienced by people as a consequence of a business, project, program, or intervention (State of New South Wales, 2023). The social impact categories are defined in Table 1.

A Practical Guide to Social Impact Assessment

Table 1 Social impact categories

Way of Life
- how people live, e.g., how they get around, access to adequate housing
- how people work, for example, access to adequate employment, working conditions and/or practices
- how people play, for example, access to recreation activities
- how people interact with one another daily

Community
- composition, e.g., demographics
- cohesion, character, how it functions, resilience and sense of place

Accessibility
- access to and use of infrastructure, services and facilities whether provided by local, state, or federal governments, or by for-profit or not-for-profit organisations or volunteer groups

Culture
- shared beliefs, customs, values and stories, and connections to land, places, and buildings (including Aboriginal culture and connection to country).

Health and well-being
- physical health, e.g., asthma, lung disease, heart disease
- mental health, e.g., depression, anxiety
- wellbeing, for example, happiness and life satisfaction

Surroundings
- access to and use of ecosystem services
- access to and use of the natural and built environment, and its aesthetic value and/or amenity

Public safety
- public safety and security e.g., crime, accidents and incidents, exposure to communicable or harmful chemicals.

Livelihoods
- economic e.g., employment, revenue
- personal disadvantage
- civil liberties

Decision-making
- extent to which people have a say in decisions that affect their lives
- access to complaint, remedy and grievance mechanisms.

Source: (State of New South Wales, 2023a; Vanclay, 2003)

Aspirations and concerns are not necessarily impacts; however, they inform impacts. Definitions are important:

- Social issue: "[A] state of affairs that negatively affects the personal or social lives of individuals or the well-being of communities or larger groups within a society and about which there is usually public disagreement as to its nature, causes, or solution." (Kulik, 2024)
- Social impact: Is a consequence or change that may be experienced by people because of a business, project, program or intervention (State of New South Wales, 2023).

Adopting these definitions allows you to differentiate a social impact as a direct consequence of the business, project, program or intervention as opposed to a pre-existing social issue. A pre-existing social issue does not mean that it cannot be a social impact, it just means that the business, project, program or intervention you are assessing is not causing the social issue, rather it may exacerbate an existing problem.

2.6 Role of social impact practitioner

The role of the social impact practitioner in delivery of the SIA is to:

- Facilitate the delivery of the methodology using social science methods to determine potential social impacts, both negative and positive, and their ongoing monitoring and management.

- Ensure the SIA adheres to the good practice principles as well as meeting the regulatory requirements for the jurisdiction(s) to which the project is subject.

- Provide an impartial analysis of the data and information supported by evidence to inform the decision makers.

Remember that the SIA is about informed decision making and as such, the role is not to advocate, be a champion, or to be partisan.

2.7 Other roles in delivery of SIA

As an SIA practitioner you will need to be working to deliver one component of a larger body of work and as such are part of the larger EIS team. The delivery of the SIA will be relying on inputs from a variety of sources, especially when part of an EIS. A brief description of the various roles that an SIA practitioner will need to work with:

- **Proponent:** meet the regulatory requirements set out by the jurisdiction in which the project is to be delivered. This will include procurement of technical experts to conduct feasibility studies.

- **Government:** administers the legislative and regulatory processes for the approval of proposed projects in their jurisdiction. This includes assessment of applications and the supporting technical reports.

- **Engineering:** designing, developing, and implementing the technical infrastructure for the project.

- **EIS approvals lead:** provide the project management, facilitation and oversight of the EIS to ensure deliverables are met on time and meet the regulatory requirements within the allocated budget.

- **Technical experts:** conduct technical studies that assess the feasibility and impact of the project for their area of expertise. These may include air, aquatic ecology, biosecurity, climate, coastal, contaminated land, groundwater, land use, matters of national environmental significance, noise and vibration, Indigenous and non-Indigenous cultural heritage, regulated structures, rehabilitation, traffic and transport, waste management, and water.

- **Project communications lead:** to conduct stakeholder engagement relevant to the project including project descriptions and other communications materials, negotiations, public relations and complaints management (Government - Office of the Coordinator-General, 2018)

- **EIS community and stakeholder engagement lead:** to meet the statutory stakeholder notification and consultation requirements of the EIS process.

2.8 Evidence base for determining and assessing social impacts

Determining social impacts can be complex and requires consideration of a wide range of data, information and research to support the identification and assessment of social impacts as well as the strategies for their management. This will include both primary and secondary data sources.

2.8.1 Primary data sources

Primary data can be understood as original data collected for a research study, in this case a social impact assessment study. The primary data collected, qualitative or quantitative, is designed to answer a research question(s) or support or reject research hypotheses of a study (Kim, 2017). In a social impact assessment this may include any data you collect yourself from in-depth interviews, surveys, questionnaires, focus groups, or workshops.

2.8.2 Secondary data sources

Secondary data refers to data that has already been collected by others and is available for use. The sources may include books, reports (government, private, not for profits), journal articles, diaries, technical reports, government records, and websites, etc.

2.9 Community and Stakeholder Engagement in SIA

One last thing before we dive into the SIA methodology and its application. I want to clarify the role of community and stakeholder engagement (CSE) in assessing social impacts. Engagement of communities and stakeholders is an important component in assessing impacts and will occur alongside and as part of an SIA.

When conducting an SIA as part of an environmental impact statement (EIS) or environmental and social impact

2 Foundations of Social Impact Assessment

statement (ESIA) there will be requirements for CSE that are broader than the SIA scope of works. In these scenarios examine the range, quantity and quality of engagement both as a stand-alone key matter and as a component of other key social issues (Government Office of the Coordinator-General, 2023).

In an SIA process, CSE is important for understanding the social context, assessing potential social impacts, and developing mitigation and enhancement strategies and measures. The CSE objectives during the SIA process may include:

TIPS

People are the best experts of their own experience. They provide intel about the local area, culture, way of life and aspirations. Different groups may need different strategies for communication and require adoption of different methodologies.

- Providing a better understanding of the values, knowledge and experiences of the different community and stakeholder groups.

- Providing an opportunity to validate and verify secondary data.

- Helping the potentially impacted communities and stakeholders understand the project and its implications.

- Helping improve project design (Government Office of the Coordinator-General, 2023).

- Giving stakeholders and the community confidence that their concerns and perspectives are being considered early in the assessment.

- Understanding of community sentiment and reduce the risk of delays from unexpected community responses or unforeseen impacts.

- Creating better proponent-community relations and more socially sustainable outcomes (State of New South Wales, 2023a).

3 Costing a Social Impact Assessment

This section will step you through how to cost an SIA.

3.1 Request for Proposal

You just received a request for proposal (RFP) to conduct an SIA for a wind farm from Super Power Pty Ltd to support an environmental planning approval in NSW, Australia.

Using the RFP provided in Table 2, you will need to:

- Determine the regulatory requirements and standards for the SIA
- Determine a study area and/or area of social influence
- Identify potentially affected communities
- Identify potential vulnerable groups and locations
- Determine an appropriate methodology
- Identify resources for delivery of the SIA
- Propose a timeline for delivery
- Provide a costing
- Demonstrate your capability and capacity to deliver the SIA
- Write the fee proposal.

A Practical Guide to Social Impact Assessment

Table 2 Request for Proposal

Offshore Windfarm – Request for Proposal

Super Power Pty Ltd is seeking approval to conduct and operate the Super Wind Farm (the Project), a renewable energy project located east of in the Southern Tablelands region of NSW. The proponent is seeking State Significant Development (SSD) consent under the Environmental Planning & Assessment Act 1979 (EP&A Act) for the Project.

Project Overview

Super Power proposes to develop the Super Wind Farm near the town of Torago, in the Southern Tablelands Region located on the Goulburn-Braidwood road. The Project Area is situated approximately 222 km southwest of Sydney located in the Goulbourn Mulwaree Local Government Area (LGA). Part of the defined locality, which includes a large area of grazing country, is on the eastern shore of Lake George in the Queanbeyan-Palerang Regional Council. The town is situated 39 km south of the city of Goulbourn and 69 km northeast of Canberra, the capital city of Australia (Wikipedia 2023).

The Project Proposed wind farm will consist of up to 176 wind turbine generators with an estimated maximum installed capacity of up to approximately 1,003 MW. The wind turbines will have a proposed hub height of 291.5 m. The Project proposes to use Nordex turbines.

Large scale battery storage is also proposed to supply electricity to the National Electricity Market (NEM). The Project involves the construction of a Battery Energy Storage System facility with a capacity of up to 200 MW/800 MWh. It will be located in the south of the Project Area and would likely use lithium ion technology.

Project supporting infrastructure and associated work will include:

3 Costing a Social Impact Assessment

- One operations and maintenance facility (located at one of the substations)
- Up to three substations (north, south and central)
- Up to two temporary concrete batching plants (located at one of the substations)
- Possible onsite temporary crushing facilities
- One switching station
- Four temporary and four permanent meteorological monitoring masts with a height of 160m
- Wind turbine hardstands
- Overhead and underground electrical cabling
- Construction laydown areas and compounds
- Security fencing and landscaping
- Internal access tracks, site access and road upgrades along the haulage route (as required)
- Ancillary activities including gravel pits, water sourcing, visual screening (as required)
- Temporary worker accommodation.

3.1.1 Step 1: Determine the regulatory requirements and standards for the SIA

The Request for Proposal states that the project is located in the State of NSW and that Super Power are seeking consent for SSD under the EP&A Act.

It is important to understand that government is responsible for the decision making and oversight of the approvals process. When responding to the RFP it is important to understand which government department is responsible for oversight of the approvals for the project. The approval process and related requirements usually include guidelines and/or standards. For example, in NSW the Department of Planning and Environment (DPE) has responsibility for sustainable planning in NSW. DPE has published a *Social Impact Assessment Guideline, February 2023* (NSW SIA Guideline) outlining the requirements for a SIA for a state significant development as well as a Technical Supplement and SIA Scoping Worksheet. The links to these documents can be found here:

- Social Impact Assessment Guideline: https://www.planningportal.nsw.gov.au/Social-Impact-Assessment

- Technical Supplement and SIA Scoping Worksheet: https://www.planningportal.nsw.gov.au/Social-Impact-Assessment

3 Costing a Social Impact Assessment

Consider if there are other relevant International Guidance or Standards e.g.:

> **TIPS**
>
> Develop a checklist of all the mandatory and non-mandatory requirements.
>
> You can use this to ensure your SIA has met all requirements.

* The IAIA SIA Guidance is available online: https://www.iaia.org/uploads/pdf/SIA_Guidance_Document_IAIA.pdf

* The IFC have issued Performance Standards on Environmental and Social Sustainability, Effective January 1, 2012, available online: https://www.ifc.org/en/insights-reports/2012/ifc-performance-standards

* United Nations 17 Sustainable Development Goals, which can be found here: https://sdgs.un.org.

Once you have the guidance document(s) you can apply them through the steps below.

3.1.2 Step 2 Identify potentially affected communities

Potentially affected communities are those who will likely be directly and indirectly affected by the project.

To identify potentially affected communities involves identifying anyone interested in the project or process. Large projects, such as infrastructure projects, often attract a lot of

27

community interest and their impacts far reaching. There are two broad categories of stakeholders, those who contribute to a project and those who are affected by a project.

Analysis of the stakeholders involves consideration of the potential sensitivity, impact and outrage the project may generate against the complexity of the project. This is done by mapping stakeholder against the matrix shown in Figure 2. Depending on where stakeholders fall on the matrix informs the level of engagement required.

Prioritisation of the stakeholder's communication and engagement needs is incorporated in the matrix in Figure 2. Those who are assessed as low need to be kept informed; medium need to be consulted and/or involved; and high need to be engaged using collaborative and/or empowerment methods.

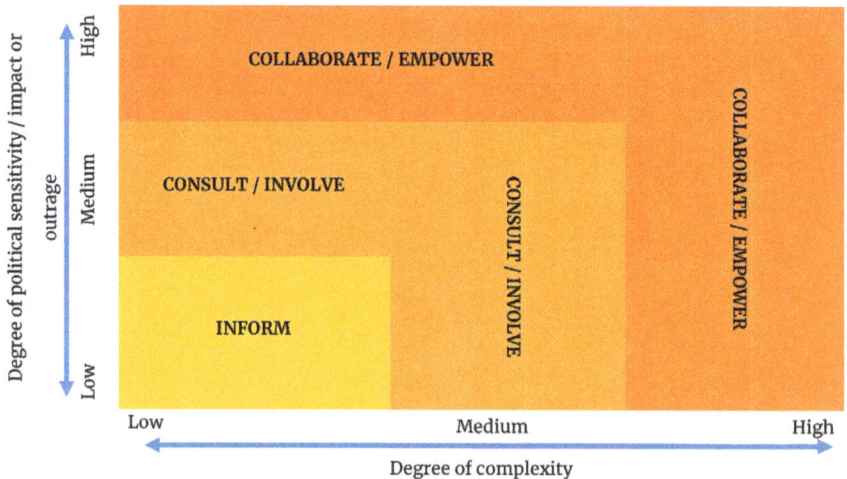

Source: International Association for Public Participation, 2018
Figure 2 Stakeholder matrix

3 Costing a Social Impact Assessment

TIPS

The EIS project team may have a community and engagement professional to do the EIS engagement. If so, work with them to ensure the SIA stakeholders and EIS engagement are integrated.

Engagement with stakeholders should be aligned with the needs of each stakeholder group allowing the management of risk and maximisation of outcomes of the project. The IAP2 public participation spectrum (Table 3) is used to guide engagement activities.

Table 3 IAP2 Spectrum of public participation

	Public participation goal	Methods of engagement
INFORM	To provide the public with balanced and objective information to assist them in understanding the problems, alternatives and/or solutions.	• Fact sheets • Websites • Open houses
CONSULT	To obtain public feedback on analysis, alternatives and/or decisions.	• Public comment • Focus groups • Surveys • Public meetings
INVOLVE	To partner with the public in each aspect of the decision including the development of alternatives and the identification of the preferred solution.	• Facilitated workshops • Deliberate polling
COLLABORATE	To partner with the public in each aspect of the decision including the development and the identification of the preferred solution.	• Citizen advisory committees • Consensus building • Participatory decision-making
EMPOWER	To place final decision-making in the hands of the public.	• Citizen juries • Ballots • Delegated decisions

Source: Adapted from International Association for Public Participation, 2018

3 Costing a Social Impact Assessment

Potentially affected communities may include:

❖ Directly affected:

- Residents both local and regional e.g., town(s) and /or suburb(s) closest to the proposed project site, along transport routes and the supply chain.

- Land use of neighbouring properties e.g., residential, farming, business, services (schools, hospitals, emergency services etc).

- Workforce

- First Nations people

❖ Indirectly affected:

- National, state and local authorities

- Neighbouring projects

- Nongovernmental organisations (International Finance Corporation (IFC), 2012)

Ongoing monitoring and evaluation are achieved by developing and maintaining an issues register for the life of the project. This will allow for monitoring stakeholder sentiment, responding to issues as they arise, re-prioritisation of stakeholders if required and adapt engagement methods where appropriate.

A Practical Guide to Social Impact Assessment

Provide a snapshot of the communities that are potentially impacted, that includes:

- Total population and population by locality/suburb and LGA including First Nations people

- Male and female population

- Age distribution (population pyramid)

- Migrant population

- Unemployment

- Top three industries of employment

- Highest level of education

- Socio economic advantage and disadvantage indexes (SEIFA) used in Australia.

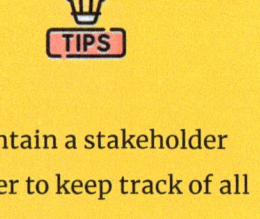

Maintain a stakeholder register to keep track of all engagement activities.

 3.1.3 Step 3 Determine the SIA study area

This is a geographic physical boundary for your SIA study. To determine the SIA study area you will need to use a mapping tool such as Google Maps or Google Earth. Use the location provided in the RFP to find the proposed Project site location.

3 Costing a Social Impact Assessment

To assist in determining how far from the project site the SIA study will be you should consider the activities of the project and the distance from the site likely impacts (e.g., related to dust, noise, transport and traffic, surface water, groundwater etc) will be experienced by community (including businesses) and affect infrastructure and services.

Articulate the geographic extent to which the Project will have an impact. Consider supply chain, trucks movements to and from site, workforce movements and accommodations

Take note of the following:

TIPS

Identify both a local and regional area of influence. Local being those more directly impacted and regional indirectly.

- Town(s) and/or suburb(s) closest to the proposed project site

- Local government area(s)

- Access roads and other transport routes (rail, road and air)

- Nearby regional communities that may provide workforce, materials and/or services to the Project

- Location of worker accommodation camps to house FIFO, drive-in-drive-out (DIDO) or bus-in-bus-out (BIBO) workforce.

3.1.4 Step 4 identify potential vulnerable groups and locations

Before commencing let's define what we mean by vulnerable. For the purpose of SIA we are wanting to identify qualities or states of people or places that make them more susceptible to harm (physically or emotionally). The IFC (2012) define disadvantage or vulnerability as an individual's or groups status stemming from their "race, colour, sex, language, religion, political or other opinion, national or social origin, property, birth, or other status." The IFC encourages client consideration of "factors such as gender, age, ethnicity, culture, literacy, sickness, physical or mental disability, poverty or economic disadvantage, and dependence on unique natural resources." (International Finance Corporation, 2012).

When determining vulnerable or marginalised groups consider the prevalence in the population of groups and their capacity to adapt and resilience to change:

- ❖ First Nations people
- ❖ People with a disability
- ❖ Homeless or at risk of homelessness
- ❖ Children

TIPS

Check the following to assist:

- Use census data
- Local Councils
- NGO's operating in the area and their target groups
- Australian Disaster Resilience Index: https://adri.bnhcrc.com.au/#!/

- Youth

- Elderly

- Land use dependency e.g., farming and agriculture

- Migrant groups and/or people who speak a language other than English at home

- Low socioeconomic status

- People with health conditions that put them at risk from project e.g., asthma, chronic obstructive pulmonary disease (COPD), anxiety, depression.

TIPS

If you are unable to conduct a site visit use google earth or google maps to see what infrastructure surrounds the project site. Remember to consider transport routes and supply chain.

When determining vulnerable locations consider if there is social infrastructure nearby the site or along transport routes that would pose a risk to community access or use of, for example:

- Hospitals or health care services

- Emergency Services

- Childcare centres

- Schools

- Safe crossings

- Places of worship

- Other social gathering places such as community halls, sporting facilities, natural reserves etc.

3.1.5 Step 5 Determine an appropriate detailed methodology

Use the information gathered in Steps 2 – 4 to help determine your proposed methodology. Use the relevant guideline and international standards for SIA to help determine your proposed methodology.

In addition to the RFP, you will need the following:

- Some form of map, e.g., geographic information system (GIS), Google Maps, or Google Earth

- SIA Guideline and other guidance and standards, and

- Regulation.

Consider the methods (online and face to face) you will adopt to collect data and information i.e. social impact survey, town resource cluster survey, site visit, in-depth interviews, workshops, focus groups discussions. Give thought to your vulnerable groups and make sure your methods are appropriate.

Take time to consider the project, its context and/or design that may inform the methods you adopt.

Remember to design a methodology that is appropriate taking into consideration elements of the project and how they relate to the location, context, stakeholders and community. The case study below demonstrates the tailoring of the SIA methodology to suit a project design, location and community context.

A Practical Guide to Social Impact Assessment

CASE STUDY
Social impact assessment of a Residual Void Project

Project

An open cut and underground bord and pillar coal mine located in Central Queensland that consists of seven pits on both sides of the Nogoa River.

The proponent prepared three design options as part of their Residual Void Project for assessment and identification of a preferred option.

Scope of works

Andrea delivered an SIA that met the requirements of the SSRC Act and supporting SIA Guideline. The approach drew on her professional experience in preparing SIAs for resource projects across Queensland and knowledge of the Central Queensland region and the Terms of Reference for the project. The methodology was informed by international good practice in SIA.

The SIA activities undertaken included:

- preparation of a social baseline and constraints
- prediction of change and trend lines, and their potential impacts for each of the three options
- evaluation of social impacts for each of the three options
- development of responses to social impacts and
- development of a SIMP.

A co-design approach was adopted with data collected via surveys, face to face, in-depth interviews with nearby neighbours and landholders and, focus groups with Traditional Owners and special interest groups, in Emerald and Rockhampton, to identify and assess the social impacts and the community and stakeholders preferred option.

Briefings were held with regional stakeholder government agencies (i.e. local, State and Federal). A stall was set up at the AgGrow Exhibition in Emerald, where project information sheets were distributed, and surveys administered. A project summary booklet, outlining the key environmental and social outcomes, was developed, and distributed to project key stakeholders.

Project challenges and strategic responses

Working closely with the proponent provided strategic advice and support. Proponent proposed two options:

- Option 1 Landform Levee: Develop permanent landforms along the existing levee alignment, to provide flood immunity for a 1 in 1,000 flood event
- Option 2 Flood Mitigation and Beneficial Use: Design some of the rehabilitated landforms to capture and store a proportion of the high-flow flood water
- Option 3 Backfilling Voids: Set by the Government Fully backfilling voids on flood plains.

The SIA and SCE activities were used to inform and adjust the designs of Options 1 and 2, to maximise benefits and minimise negative outcomes. Given the proximity of the voids to farming in the region and the Yamala Inland Port water and water quality posed a barrier to Option 1 and Option 2.

The SIA and SCE activities allowed for communication of the technical outcomes and gauging and fostering support for these options should they be viable. This resulted in Ensham to provide flood mitigation under Option 1 with the potential to revisit Option 2 when and if appropriate.

To add robustness to the process the environmental, economic and social assessment was subjected to a triple bottom line assessment and peer reviewed by the Sustainable Minerals

A Practical Guide to Social Impact Assessment

> Institute, University of Queensland. The SIA was independently peer reviewed by Dr Ana Maria Esteves, Board Member of the International Association of Impact Assessment.

Source: Conducted under umbrella of Umwelt Australia Pty Ltd

It is useful to illustrate the methodology using a diagram. Examples of how to illustrate SIA methodologies are provided in Figure 3.

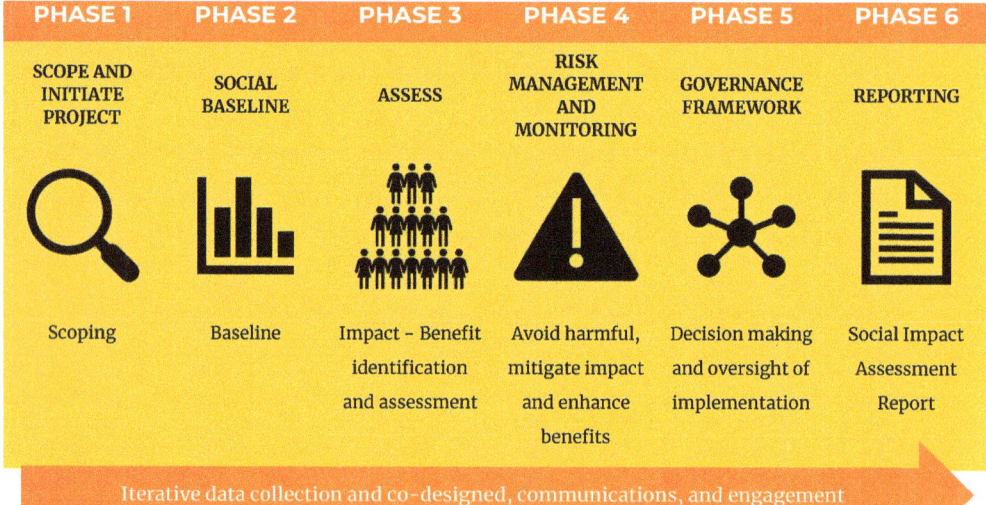

3 Costing a Social Impact Assessment

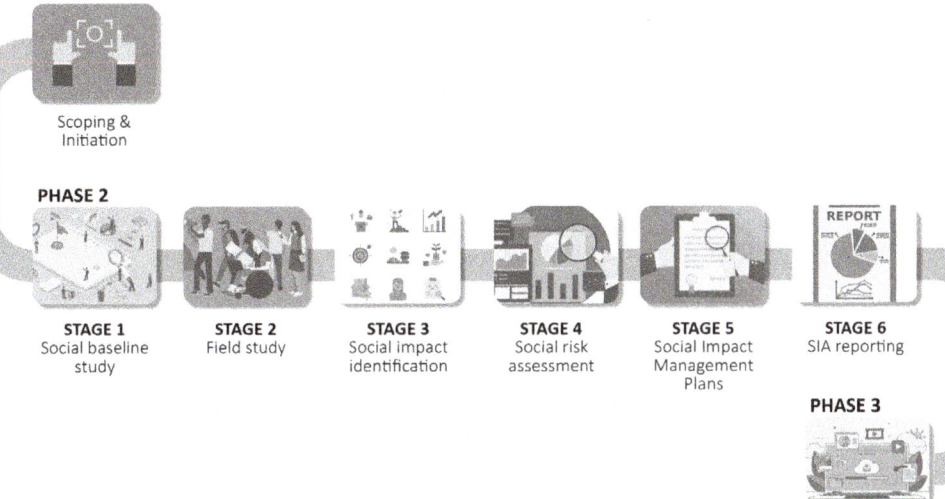

Source: Produced for EMM Consulting
Figure 3 SIA Methodologies

Once you have your illustration you can provide a more detailed breakdown of the methods. The blue text in Table 4 provides examples of activities, inputs and deliverables for various phases of the SIA that can be used in your response to the RFP.

Table 4 Detailed methods

Phase	Activity	Inputs	Deliverables
Scoping and initiation	Conduct Site visit	1 x SIA practitioner	Site visit
	Develop Project Plan	Car hire	Project Plan
			RFI
	Prepare Request for Information (RFI)	Return flight	

Phase	Activity	Inputs	Deliverables
Social Baseline	Retrieval of data (demographic, health status, crime etc)	Census data	
		Excel	
		GIS mapping	
	Service mapping		
	Data review and analysis		
	Data presentation		
Field Study	Social impact survey	Survey Monkey	Draft Social Baseline
	In depth interviews	Excel or SPSS	Final Social Baseline
	Workshops	Butchers paper	(summarised and attached to SIA Report)
	Focus Group Discussions (FGDs)		
Social risk identification	Identify social impacts based on findings from social baseline, field study, CSE and technical reports	Baseline Study	List of social impacts and benefits for assessment
		Findings SIA Field Study	
		Findings EIS and Project Consultation	Briefing to client outlining social impacts and benefits for assessment
		Technical Reports	
		Previous SIAs	
		Social Research	

3 Costing a Social Impact Assessment

Phase	Activity	Inputs	Deliverables
Social risk assessment	Apply social risk framework to each identified social impact	Baseline Study Findings SIA Field Study Findings EIS and Project Consultation Technical Reports Previous SIAs Social Research	Unmitigated risk ranking for each impact and benefit assuming Mitigated risk ranking for each impact and benefit assuming
SIMP – Mitigation and Enhancement Strategies	Develop social impact mitigation, management and enhancement strategies, and metrics	Findings from social risk assessment Pervious SIAs of similar projects Social research	Mitigation and Enhancement Framework, or Social Impact Management Plan Metrics for measurement of successful delivery of mitigation and enhancement strategies

Phase	Activity	Inputs	Deliverables
Reporting	Prepare Draft Final SIA Report	Findings from above Phases	Draft Social Impact Report
		Client Feedback Review	Final Social Impact Report
		Optional: Independent Peer Review	

Table 5 provides some guidance on the methods you can adopt to conduct your SIA field study.

Table 5 Field study method guidance

Method	Purpose	Tools	Guide
Social impact survey	To get input from local and regional residents that are indirectly affected to the identification of potential impacts	Survey Monkey or other survey tool Computer Assisted Telephone Interviewing (CATI)	Distribution can be via online platforms such as Social Pinpoint, Resident Facebook pages, Council websites, project website Hard copy distribution

3 Costing a Social Impact Assessment

Method	Purpose	Tools	Guide
Town Resource Cluster survey	To understand the potential impacts related to the supply chain e.g. service providers and businesses in regional resource centres	Survey Monkey or other survey tool CATI	Can be administered through direct emails, hard copy distribution or in person
Site visit	Determine SIA study area and understand the surrounding area of social influence. Understand the proximity of proposed site to landholders, residents, social infrastructure and recreational areas	Induction online & onsite Health, Safety and Environment (HSE) planning Personal protection equipment (PPE)	SIA Lead should be in attendance during scoping phase

Method	Purpose	Tools	Guide
In depth interviews	To determine the potential impacts on those directly affected e.g., landholders and nearby neighbours, Council representatives, and First Nations representatives and Native Title Claimants, special interest groups	Detailed project description and maps Stakeholder list, including contact details Interview guides Booking sheet Booking transcript Transcription of interviews	Face to Face Online (Teams or Zoom)
Workshops	To determine potential impact on directly affected service providers (health, emergency, childcare, education, employment, real estate, accommodation) and businesses.	Detailed project description and maps Stakeholder list, including contact details Facilitator Scribe Butchers paper and pens Red and Green dots	Face to Face Online (Teams or Zoom)

Method	Purpose	Tools	Guide
Focus Group Discussions (FGDs)	To determine potential impact on a specific group of directly affected stakeholders that have similar interests and concerns.	FGD Guide	Facilitated group discussion (ideally Face to Face)
Social impact survey	To get input from local and regional residents that are indirectly affected to the identification of potential impacts	Survey Monkey or other survey tool CATI	Online platforms such as Social Pinpoint, Resident Facebook pages, Council websites, project website Hard copy distribution
Town Resource Cluster survey	To understand the potential impacts related to the supply chain e.g. service providers and businesses in regional resource centres	Survey Monkey or other survey tool CATI	Direct emails Hard copy distribution In person or telephone

3.1.6 Step 6 Identify resources for delivery of the SIA

Resources will include people, your team, and any tools you made need to deliver the SIA.

When identifying team members consider the complexity of the Project and the skills needed to deliver the SIA such as:

- Qualitative and quantitative data collection, management and analysis.

- Interpretation and presentation of data.

- Facilitation skills if conducting workshops or focus groups.

- In-depth interview skills.

- Social risk assessment.

- Social impact and benefit assessment.

- Social impact management and enhancement strategies.

- Interpretation of findings from technical reports.

- GIS mapping.

- Report writing.

- Project / study management.

Other resources you will need to consider:

* Data collection and management systems, some may require subscriptions.

* CATI services for telephone surveys.

* Travel which may include air fares, care hire, accommodation, meals, incidentals.

* CSE activities that may require venue hire, refreshments, flip charts, pens, printing of communications collateral (information sheets, flyers etc), scribing, transcription.

3.1.7 Step 7 Propose a timeline for delivery

Once you have articulated the methodology including activities, team members and other resources you will need to determine how long it will take to deliver. The timeframe will be informed by the RFP and complexity of SIA.

For each stage of your methodology determine when key milestones will be delivered. A Gantt chart (Figure 4) is a useful way to provide the timeframe for delivery. You may also use a table format (Table 6).

If you have been provided a commencement date you can use it to develop a timeline. If you do not have a date for commencement, I suggest outlining a proposed timeline e.g. specifying deliverables against each week.

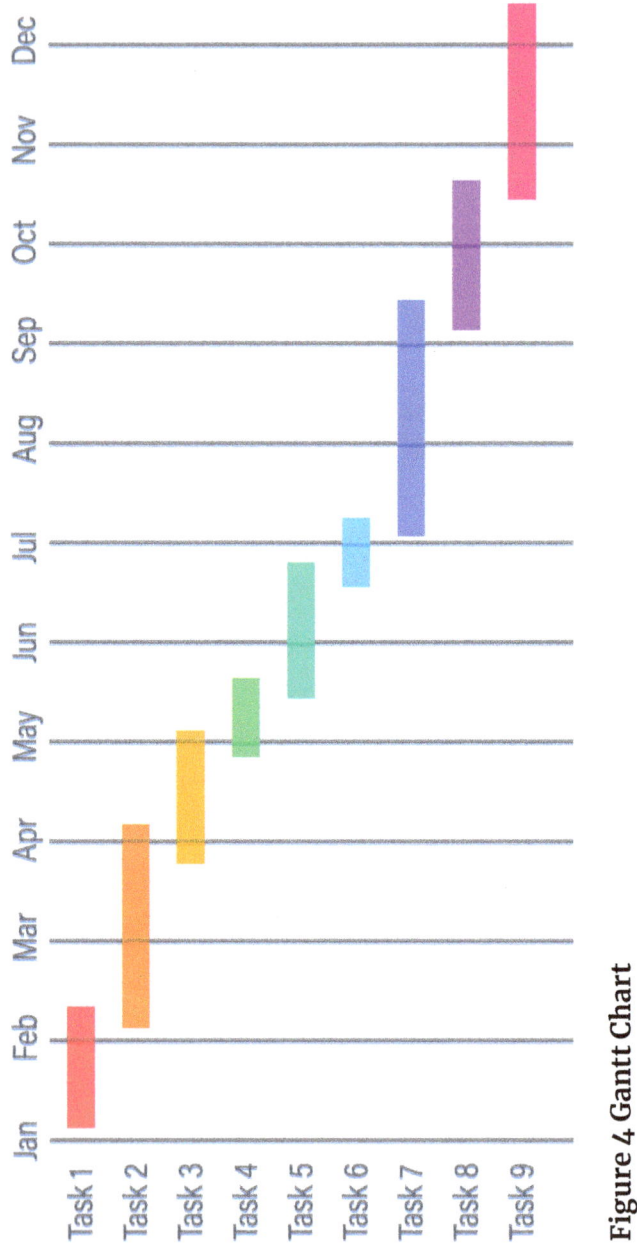

Figure 4 Gantt Chart

3 Costing a Social Impact Assessment

Table 6 Timeframe for delivery

Phase	Deliverable	Timeframe
Scoping and inception	• Kick off meeting and site visit • PPP	• Early August 2025
Social Baseline	• Social locality • Draft social baseline • Final social baseline	• Late August 2025 • Mid-September 2025 • End September 2025
Field Study	• Data collection and analysis	• October – November 2025
Social impact identification	• Briefing on identified social impacts for assessment	• Early December 2025
Social impact – benefit assessment	• Risk – benefit assessment workshop	• December 2025
Social impact management plan	• Draft SIMP / Framework	• January 2026
Reporting	• Draft SIA Report • Final SIA Report	• February 2026 • March 2026
Study management	• Progress reporting • Invoice	• Monthly August 2025 – March 2026

51

 ### 3.1.8 Step 8 Costing

Now you have your methodology, resources and timeframes it is time to cost your SIA.

To allow you to cost each task you will need to decide the hourly rate for each of your team members and include it in your response to the RFP. An example of how you may present this information is provided in Table 7.

Table 7 Project team hourly rates

Project team role	Hourly Rate
Study/Project Director	$XXX.XX
Study/Project Manager	$XXX.XX
SIA Lead	$XXX.XX
SIA Consultant	$XXX.XX
SIA Assistant	$XXX.XX
GIS Specialist	$XXX.XX

Calculate your human hours:

'number of hours to complete task' x 'hourly rate'

Repeat for each task. Remember to include time for travel, meetings and project management.

In some instances, you may need to use more than one person to complete a task. Using an Excel Spreadsheet like that shown in Figure 5 can assist in making these calculations easier.

3 Costing a Social Impact Assessment

CLIENT NAME : SuperPower
PROJECT NAME : Super Wind Farm

DESCRIPTION	HRLY RATE	$ 180.00	$ 120.00	$ 150.00
	FEE	SIA Lead	Consultant	GIS
Scoping	$690	1	3	1
Social Baseline	$2,940	4	16	2
Field Study	$6,720	16	32	
Data analysis and review	$2,880		24	
Impact Identification	$1,500	3	8	
Impact Assessment	$2,040	6	8	
Mitigation and Management Framework	$2,640	4	16	
Reporting	$6,930	16	30	3
Project Management	$2,160	12		
Total Hours for Phase PER PERSON	205	62	137	6
Total Cost for Phase PER PERSON	$ 28,500.00	$ 11,160.00	$ 16,440.00	$ 900.00

Figure 5 Fee calculator

When allocating team members to tasks you will need to be thinking practically about how you will deliver the project, therefore, consider the scale and complexity of the project. Doing so will help to determine which skills are required to deliver each of the tasks and how many people needed for delivery. Below are a couple of examples that will help you to think it through:

TIPS

Consider if the project is likely to attract attention from activist groups, are there known contentions / impacts related to the project or similar projects that are likely to affect the community and is it politically sensitive?

53

- Scoping the project might require some experience, so perhaps your SIA Lead will be the right person. Or, you might need a map to show the location of the project site and the surrounding towns/suburbs and local government areas, this would require GIS mapping.

- Baseline data will require the ability to understand and interpret demographic data, health data and other social data (e.g., crime data, emergency services, housing and accommodation data etc). This may require a demographer or social scientist.

- Field study activities adopted will need to align to the level of effort, e.g., if you are conducting in person workshops and in-depth interviews in Tarago, NSW you will need to document the discussions and findings from the workshops. This means you will need e.g., a scribe, a recorder, and transcription. Table 3 provides guidance on all the inputs you will need for each activity.

- Data analysis and review

- Social impact identification

- Social impact and benefit assessment

- Social impact mitigation

- Reporting

- Submissions

3 Costing a Social Impact Assessment

Each team member should have an hourly rate that you use to help calculate the overall fee for the SIA. Those hourly rates can be entered into a fee calculator like that shown in Figure 3. Doing so will help you to have a detailed breakdown of the SIA with time allocated to each phase and its related activities. This is very helpful for building a total fee estimate but also for determining delivery timeframes and tracking the progress once you win the contract. For the response to the RFP you submit to the client, I recommend using the table shown in Table 8.

Table 8 Fee estimate

Activity	Hours	Total (Excluding GST)
Stage 1: E.g., Scoping and inception	XX	$X,XXX.XX
E.g., Kick off meeting and site visit	XX	$X,XXX.XX
Stage 2: E.g., Social Baseline	XX	$X,XXX.XX
E.g., Identify the project's social locality	XX	$X,XXX.XX
Stage 3: E.g., Field Study	XX	$X,XXX.XX
E.g., In-depth interviews, workshops, focus groups	XX	$X,XXX.XX
Stage 4: E.g., Identify social impacts	XX	$X,XXX.XX
E.g., Review technical studies	XX	$XX,XXX.XX
Stage 5: E.g., Social risk assessment	XX	$X,XXX.XX
E.g., Risk workshop (unmitigated & residual)	XX	$X,XXX.XX

A Practical Guide to Social Impact Assessment

Activity	Hours	Total (Excluding GST)
Stage 6: E.g., Mitigation and management	XX	$X,XXX.XX
E.g., Develop management framework	XX	$X,XXX.XX
Stage 7: E.g., Reporting	XX	$X,XXX.XX
E.g., Draft SIA report	XX	$X,XXX.XX
E.g., Final SIA report	XX	$X,XXX.XX
Project Management and Coordination	XX	$X,XXX.XX
E.g., Project plan, RFI, monthly reporting	XX	$X,XXX.XX
TOTAL EXCLUDING GST	XX	$X,XXX.XX
GST (10%)	–	$X,XXX.XX
TOTAL	XX	$X,XXX.XX

3.1.8.1 Inclusions and exclusions

You will need to make sure you articulate the assumptions made, i.e., what is included and excluded, to calculate your fee to deliver the proposed methodology. For example, some of the most common inclusions and exclusions include:

- ❖ If you are conducting a site visit, have you included the cost of travel and accommodation related expenses?

- ❖ During field study have you included cost of hiring venues for workshops/focus groups and refreshments?

- Have you assumed that data and information will be provided in a useable format?

- Have you included the cost of data collection and management subscriptions?

3.1.8.2 Deliverables and timeframe

You will need to clearly list the deliverables at each stage and the timeline for delivery. There is an opportunity to integrate this into the information provided in Table 7.

 **3.1.9 Step 9 Demonstrate your capability and capacity to deliver the SIA.**

When detailing your experience remember to try to tailor the information to the RFP. You will need:

- A pitch that outlines your or your companies' capabilities and skills

- Project examples

- CVs and membership in professional bodies for key team members

- References may be required for some large-scale projects

3.1.10 Step 10 Write your Response to RFP

Using the information from Step 1 – 9 prepare a document, either letter or report format, to submit to the proponent.

The potential headings for your proposal may consist of:

1. Background

   a. Includes any significant activities related to the project e.g., previous iterations of the project, previous approvals and engagement activities.

2. Project appreciation:

   a. Location of the project

   b. Relevant approvals process and current phase

   c. Related regulatory requirements

3. Methodology / Scope of works:

   a. Includes the proposed methodology

   b. Activities and deliverables that meet the regulatory requirements

   c. Timeframe for delivery

4. Why [insert your company name]:

    a. Includes a pitch of why they should choose you

    b. Brief introduction to key team members. Attach CVs to the fee proposal. attached to your fee proposal

5. Fee estimate:

    a. Includes the breakdown of your fees as shown in Table 8.

    b. Table 8 and below the table provide assumptions, inclusions and exclusions

    a. Hourly rates of all your team members for any additional work that may be required

4 Conducting a Social impact Assessment

Congratulations! Super Power have awarded you the contract and now it is time to deliver the SIA.

First thing you need to do is prepare for the initiation meeting where you will need to:

- Confirm your methodology.

- Clarify timeframe for delivery, including any dates for field trip(s).

- Clarify roles and responsibilities.

- Clarify how the project team will communicate with the client.

- Prepare and provide a request for information.

 ## 4.1 Phase 1 Scoping and initiation

The information provided in the RFP should form the basis of scoping the SIA study area, identification of vulnerable groups and potential social risks for investigation.

Proper administration of the SIA will be key to delivering on time, within budget and to the standard required. Let's make sure you have what we need to manage the study. You should have:

A Practical Guide to Social Impact Assessment

- ❖ Schedule for delivery, e.g., a Gantt chart will assist you to track the progress of your deliverables against their due date and identify overlaps with activities in the SIA and will assist in discussions with EIS project team about interdependencies.

- ❖ Regular team meetings (SIA team and broader project team) to help keep project on track and to identify risks early.

- ❖ Reporting mechanisms and timeframes e.g., monthly written reports to accompany monthly invoice.

Interdependencies are those technical studies findings which inform the assessment of social impacts (e.g., air quality, acoustics, transport, water quality, cultural heritage etc) and therefore need to precede some of the SIA activities.

- ❖ Issue and risk management.

The first thing you will need to do is prepare for the initiation meeting and site visit. This will include:

1. Confirming the date and time of the initiation meeting.

2. Drafting a project protocols plan for discussion and clarification in the initiation meeting.

3. Organising a site visit, including knowing who you will be meeting and where:

4 Conducting a Social impact Assessment

- Book flights, accommodation and car hire as required.

- Prepare a journey safety assessment (JSA).

- Arrange for appropriate PPE.

Consider the effects of fatigue related to your travel and factor in breaks for long trips.

Check with your client about their fatigue management plan or use local fatigue management guidelines to inform your JSA.

4.2 Phase 2 SIA delivery

This section outlines how you will deliver the SIA stage by stage.

 ### 4.2.1 Stage 1 Social Baseline

A social baseline is a snapshot of time that identifies the current conditions, allowing for measuring change caused by the project or intervention. You will need to source publicly available data on the population in your area of social influence. In some jurisdictions you will have access to adequate publicly available demographic, health, crime and social service data. In other jurisdictions you may need to conduct household surveys to obtain the population data you need.

When conducting your analysis of the data consider the proposed activities the project will undertake and the risks inherent in the project at each phase i.e., prefeasibility, construction, operational, closure and post-closure (Table 9). The SIA is for the purpose of seeking approval so that would mean the SIA is being conducted as part of the feasibility studies.

Remember to interpret the data, highlight what the data is telling you about the community/ies. A useful question to ask about the data is "so what?". A baseline compiles and analyses a lot of data and asking this question will help to focus on the data sets that matter for the community/ies being studied.

4 Conducting a Social impact Assessment

Table 9 Project phases

Prefeasibility	Feasibility	Construction	Operation	Closure	Post-closure
Involves conducting a financial analysis based on reasonable assumptions. Includes exploration, prefeasibility studies.	Development of processing routes and technical, economic and socio-environmental feasibility studies. The feasibility study is intended to ascertain the potential for the development of and the scale of the project.	Construction and preparation activities relating to the development and the necessary infrastructure and includes acquisition of land and implementation of compensatory programs.	The production stage, and may include expansions, changes of process, new exploration activities, and project management.	Starts shortly before end of operations and is completed with the removal of all unnecessary facilities and implementation of actions to ensure the area is secure and stable, including reclamation and social programs.	After full implementation of decommissioning, includes monitoring, maintenance, temporary or permanent care and social programs aimed at achieving closure objectives.
Due diligence and social risk assessment	Social impact assessment	SIMP implementation	Monitoring and social impact management reporting	Delivery of social programs	

4.2.1.1 SIA Study area and social area of influence

You will need to expand on the snapshot you provided in the fee proposal. Start with developing the demographic profile of potentially affected communities, which should include:

- Population by local and regional areas, population projections, age and sex, median age, rate of homelessness.

- Socioeconomic status: median monthly and/or weekly income, unemployment rate, education level.

- Housing and accommodation: ownership vs rental, monthly mortgage and rental payments.

- Health status e.g., physical, mental and emotional.

- First Nations population including age and sex, unemployment, income and other available demographic and socioeconomic status data sets.

- Provide an analysis of community characteristics and wellbeing such as:

TIPS

In Australia you will have access to the Socio-Economic Indexes for Areas (SEIFA). Specifically, the Index of Relative Socio-Economic Advantage and Disadvantage (IRSAD) which summarises information on economic and social conditions of people and households.

- Community culture and values e.g. volunteering, religious background, cultural background

- Community history e.g. Indigenous and non-indigenous history

- Community wellbeing e.g., crime rates, mortality, living conditions, cost of living, volunteering

The Australian Bureau of Statistics, Census data includes data on voluntary and unpaid work. This incorporates care for children, disabled, aged persons and voluntary work at an organisation or group.

- Land/property ownership and utilisation of natural resources

- Household size and composition.

❖ Provide an overview of land use and key industries in the region, as well as relevant local and state government plans.

❖ Provide a profile of the local and regional market, including an assessment of the likely availability of personnel with skills relevant to the project.

❖ Detail publicly accessible information about other resources and social infrastructure such as roads, public transport, health, schools and universities, emergency services (police, ambulance, fire), community services, sporting facilities, parks and reserves, cultural facilities such as churches, community halls, art galleries etc.

- Details on other projects in the area, both planned and currently operating.

4.2.1.2 Vulnerable groups and social infrastructure

You will need to:

- Determine the individuals and/or groups, businesses, places and services that are vulnerable to effects of the project activities.

- Identify the capacity of vulnerable individuals and groups capacity to respond and/or adapt to change and to participate in the SIA.

- Identify current capacity and accessibility of infrastructure, facilities, and services such as education, health and emergency services.

- Provide an analysis of the existing housing and accommodation market, including availability, capacity, and affordability.

You will also need primary data to validate existing public data and determine the current conditions and capacity of existing social services such as health, emergency, housing etc.

4 Conducting a Social impact Assessment

When collecting primary data about the capacity of services, remember to ask about workforce availability, vacant positions and how long they remain vacant. Also, consider inter-related issues e.g., is there sufficient housing or accommodation for critical workers in the area.

This is a great time to consider your methodology and whether with greater understanding of the project, the social baseline data and potentially site visit have provided insights that can inform the approach. The case study below demonstrates how adjustments can be made not just to the SIA but other components of the EIS.

CASE STUDY

Social impact assessment of Gold Mine

Project

The Gold Mine Project State Significant Development (the Project) is an amalgamation of underground mining deposits and development of new underground workings of deposits to create the new Project.

The proponent owns and operates the Gold Mines located in far western NSW.

Scope of works

Delivered an SIA informed by best practice guidance and standards set out by the IAIA and IFC and developed in accordance with the NSW Department of Planning, Industry and Environment Social impact assessment guideline: For State significant mining, petroleum production and extractive industry development, September 2017 (DPE 2017). The assessment of the social impacts considered a range of complex factors and often competing interests. The impact assessment is reflective of this and has:

- assessed some aspects of the project as both negative and positive as they relate to different groups of people
- included negative impacts on local communities while documenting the benefits to the broader region
- identified management strategies to maximise identified benefits and mitigate and minimise negative impacts
- considered the impacts on vulnerable groups and provided management strategies to ensure that any existing disadvantages are not exacerbated, and
- considered each community's access to critical resources, such as housing and health care, and how this affects their resilience.

The town with a declining population and the decision by proponent to use a fly in fly out workforce based in workers accommodation and created a tense relationship with the community and low levels of trust. This was compounded by concerns of potential contamination from a vent rise and knowledge of the lead issue at Broken Hill and ongoing complaints about damage to property because of blasting.

Social licence to operate outcomes

Worked closely with the proponent to develop a SIA and CSE program that informed the community about the project and allowed, where possible to mitigate risk and potential impacts during the feasibility studies.

Early engagement with community identified locations which caused serious concerns about potential lead contamination across the town such as schools, kindergartens, community gardens, parks and playgrounds and front yards. Took this information back to the human health risk assessment team to ensure soil testing was taken from all the community identified locations. Those sample locations were made publicly available on the project site. In addition, proponent moved the vent rise in response to concerns

The proponents had long-term issue with stakeholder complaints about damage to her property due to vibration from blasting. The complaints were not supported by the findings of the technical reports. Regular and ongoing communications with the landholder including bringing proponents' staff and technical experts to hear directly from the landholder.

The transparency and actions taken resulted in an improved relationship and SLO demonstrated by minimal submissions made during the exhibition period.

Source: Conducted under umbrella of EMM Consulting Pty Ltd

4.2.1.3 Directly and indirectly impacted

Detail the capacity of potentially affected people to participate in the field study and community stakeholder engagement activities.

4.2.1.4 Retrieving data

If you are in Australia, you will be able to retrieve the relevant data from a range of sources identified in Table 10. Choose trusted data sources that are relevant to your project and will inform the identification of potential impacts and provide the baseline for measurement of changes as a consequence of the project.

Table 10 Australian Data Sources

Source	Data sets	
Australian Bureau of Statistics (ABS) Census data	• Population • Age and sex • Income • Housing	• Health condition by area (suburb (SA2), LGA and State) • Local business and industry • Industry of employment
Primary Health Network	• Primary or population health data i.e. nonhospital data such as: • Allied health care • General Practice • mental health • public health • First Nations health	• population health • health workforce • digital health • aged care • alcohol and other drugs

4 Conducting a Social impact Assessment

Local Council	• Local community facilities such as halls, sporting facilities, parks etc	• Current and planned infrastructure • Local history and character
State Ambulance Service	• Services by location	
My School (Australia wide)	• Sector (Government and non-Government) by School type (Primary, Secondary, Combined, Special) by location (State and Suburb) • Teaching staff numbers • FTE teaching staff numbers • Non-teaching staff numbers • FTE non-teaching staff • Index of Community Socio-Educational Advantage (ICSEA) • ICSEA distribution compared to Australia	• Year range • Total enrolments by sex • FTE enrolments • Indigenous students • Language background other than English • Attendance rates • NAPLAN results (reading, writing, spelling, grammar, numeracy) • Finances, including fees

State Planning Department	• Planning legislation, approval process, guidelines and standards	• Development applications current and planned
Residential Tenancy Authority	• Quarterly Median rent by postcode by dwelling type	
Australian Institute of Health and Wellbeing (AIHW)	• Health conditions by LGA	

State's Department of Health and/or Local health services	• Hospitals and hospital services by location
	• Health status of population such as:
	  – Life expectancy
	  – Self-rated health
	  – Burden of disease by broad cause
	  – First Nations health burden by disease group
	  – Hospitalisations
	  – Mortality
	  – Chronic disease
	  – Cancer
	  – Mental health condition(s)
	  – Communicable disease
	  – Dental and oral health
	  – Injury
	  – Lifestyle e.g., smoking, electronic cigarettes, weight, diet, alcohol, drugs, physical activity, sun safety, immunisation, environmental factors, food safety, population screening
	  – Regional health	

State Police Service	• Criminal offences by type and location (suburb, LGA)	• Services by location
State Fire Service	• Incidents • Compliance	• Service locations

Health Direct	• Health service finder such as:
	  – GP (General practice)
	  – Psychiatry
	  – Pharmacy
	  – Vaccine clinic
		– Physiotherapy
		– Pathology
		– Hospitals
		– Urgent care

Jobs and Skills Australia (Australia, State and Regional level datasets)	• Employment projections • Labour force trends • Industries	• Occupations • Labour market

If your project is outside Australia seek out census data conducted by your relevant authorities. In some countries the level of data required may not be available. In those instances, you will need to conduct a household survey. This is best conducted by a local provider.

4.2.1.5 Data management

Before you start collecting data you will need to decide how you will collect the data so that you can develop a plan for how you manage and organise data in preparation for the analysis. Do not wait until you have the data. It is important to have a strategy in place before you start data collection.

As per the fee proposal you will be collecting both quantitative and qualitative data. The first thing we will need to decide is which tools and methods you will use for both collection and analysis. Some options are shown in Table 11. This is not a comprehensive list, and I encourage you to explore the tools available to find the most appropriate for your work and that you feel comfortable using.

Table 11 Data collection and analysis tools

Activity	Qualitative data	Quantitative data
Data Collection and Management Tools	Focus Group	Online surveys
	Workshop	Telephone surveys
	In depth interviews	CATI Services
	Telephone / Videoconference	In-person questionnaire
	Recording / Transcription	
Data Analysis	Software e.g. NVivo, Atlas TI	Excel
		SPSS
	Artificial Intelligence (AI)	AI

Once you know the tools you will be using you will need to consider in advance how you will manage the data, including the methods of analysis. For example, the format provided in Table 12 is an example data management plan.

4 Conducting a Social impact Assessment

Table 12 Example data management plan

Method	Social impact survey
Purpose	Residents who are indirectly affected to inform the identification of potential impacts
Tools	Online survey using Survey Monkey for other data collection
Distribution	Distributed to all residents within the SIA study area via letter box drop with QR code embedded in an Information sheet that introduces the project and invites residents to provide input.
Data management	Data coded in Survey monkey and downloaded to excel for analysis

Mapping of issues raised to impact category |
| Presentation | Graphs, tables |

4.2.2 Stage 2 Field Study

Field study is often time consuming, labour intensive and costly. Remember to apply the Principles of SIA in Section 1.1 to ensure your approach is proportionate. Planning is important and commencing early will allow you to manage the logistics, so your timelines do not slip.

TIPS

Field study activities provide an opportunity to draw on existing engagement conducted by the Proponent and the EIS team. Reach out to the EIS Project Manager and the Communications team to identify inputs to your collateral, existing findings from consultation activities and potential for integration of activities where appropriate.

4.2.2.1 Preparing for field study

You will need:

- ❖ Comprehensive list of participants, including contact details

- ❖ Booking tracking sheet

- ❖ Invitation email / script

Information sheet that includes a brief description of the project, introduction to you and why you are contacting them, what is and why SIA, what will you do with the data, how they can contact you.

- ❖ In-depth interview guide

- ❖ Workshop and/or focus group guide

- ❖ Data privacy and release form

- ❖ Survey questions and survey tool

- ❖ JSA and PPE for field trip(s).

> Consider the lead in time required to complete all the tasks that will allow you to deliver your field study program. Remember to consider feedback from the client and any approval of content prior to circulation or contact with potential participants.

4.2.2.1.1 Data collection and management

The methods you have adopted and agreed with the client will determine the data collection resources e.g., tools and team members you will need for the collection and management of data during your field study (see Section 2.1.5 Table 5). You are likely to require both quantitative (e.g., survey) and qualitative (e.g., in-depth interviews) data so consideration of how you will collect the data as well as manage the data is important. This will include how the data sets relate to each other and what questions are pertinent to all participants and which questions are specific to particular cohorts e.g., landowners and residents adjacent to the site may have specific concerns regarding e.g., dust, noise and visual amenity that may or may not be a concern to residents further away.

4.2.2.1.1.1 Sampling

Before rushing into the data collection be sure you have identified the sampling method you will use. The purpose of sampling in an SIA is to understand the wide range of stakeholder groups that may be potentially affected and/or have an interest in the project (Coakes & Anagnostaras, 2024). It is rarely possible to include everybody or everything in social research, how participants are selected is crucial to the reliability, validity, and legitimacy of the conclusions of

When choosing sampling methods consider that SIAs are required to include participation of directly and indirectly affected stakeholders.

SIA research (Coakes & Anagnostaras, 2024). Drawing on the demographic data and characteristics, including any vulnerabilities identified in the social baseline can help inform sampling.

Table 13 is a summary of the types of sampling methods, objectives, examples of how to use the sample and things for consideration that can be used to inform your decision on which sampling method to adopt.

Table 13 Sampling methods

Strategy	Objective	Example	Considerations
Homogeneity	To describe a particular subgroup in depth, to reduce variation, simplify analysis and facilitate group interviewing.	Selecting service providers delivering programs e.g., youth, homeless to discuss challenges and vulnerabilities to change.	Used for selecting focus group participants.
Snowball	To identify cases of interest from sampling people who know people that generally have similar characteristics who, in turn know people, also with similar characteristics.	Asking participants such as known landowners and nearby neighbours to identify residents and other community stakeholders for recruitment into the SIA.	Begins by asking key informants or well-situated people "Who knows a lot about..." (Patton, 2001 cited in Palinkas et al., 2015).

Stratified purposeful	To capture major variations rather than to identify a common core, although the latter may emerge in the analysis	Combining typical case sampling with maximum variation sampling by taking a stratified purposeful sample of directly and indirectly impacted or local and regional residents for the project or program.	This represents less than the full maximum variation sample, but more than simple typical sampling.
Purposeful random	To increase the credibility of results.	Selecting for interviews a random sample of providers to describe experiences with evidence-based practice implementation.	Not as representative of the population as a probability random sample.

Source: (Palinkas et al., 2015)

Other resources you can use to help decide on your sampling method include:

- United Nations Development Programme: https://info.undp.org/docs/pdc/Documents/BRA/Social%20Impact%20Assessment_%20analysis.pdf

* ABS: https://www.abs.gov.au/websitedbs/d3310114.nsf/home/Basic+Survey+Design+-+Sample+Design

* Deakin University: https://deakin.libguides.com/qualitative-study-designs/sampling

4.2.2.1.1.2 Safety

Field study will mean undertaking activities that may put you and/or your team members at risk. Take the time to understand the risks associated with the logistics of delivering your field study program and ensure you have a JSE in place and have the appropriate PPE. The JSE should be shared with your client, project manager and if you are in a larger organisation, with your manager.

 4.2.3 Stage 3 Data Analysis and Review

You will need to analyse both qualitative and quantitative data.

4.2.3.1 Qualitative data

There are five steps for the analysis of qualitative data as illustrated in Figure 6. The qualitative data you collected will need to be analysed to understand the themes and patterns that emerged from the in-depth interviews, workshops and focus groups.

4 Conducting a Social impact Assessment

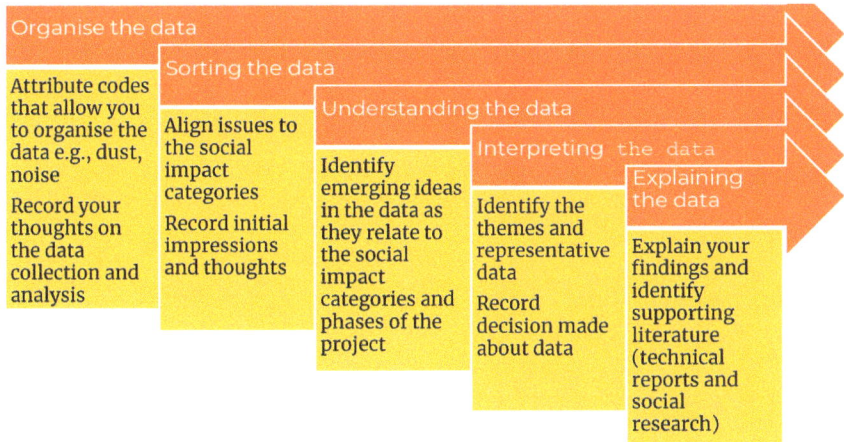

Source: Bingham, 2023
Figure 6 Data analysis process

4.2.3.2 Quantitative data

Quantitative data:

- Measures values and/or counts and is expressed as numbers.

- Is about numeric variables (e.g. how many, how much or how often) (Australian Bureau of Statistics, n.d.).

4.2.3.3 Triangulation

Triangulation is about looking at the problem from different angles. A jigsaw puzzle cannot be solved with one piece. Trying to guess what the full picture is just from that one piece, would be hard, right?

Now, what if there were three or four different pieces from different parts of the puzzle? That would help provide a much better idea of what the full picture looks like!

That's what triangulation does when conducting social research. Instead of just asking one-person, different methods or ways are used to find out the truth. These can be:

- Conducting in-depth interviews

- Conducting surveys or questionnaires

- Observational research

- Technical reports

- Reviewing academic research.

This helps in four ways:

- It makes our answers better. Different ways of collecting information help us see the full picture.

- It helps us know if something is wrong. If one source says "Yes" but another says "No," we know we need more data and information.

- It helps us confirm and validate the truth. If different sources say the same thing, we can be more confident that what the data is telling us is correct.

- It helps us discover surprises – Sometimes, looking at things from different angles shows us something we didn't expect or anticipate (Better Evaluation, 2022).

Using multiple data sources strengthens the confidence in the findings and the impact assessment. A simple triangulation matrix (Table 14) can help check that planned data collection will cover all the key field study questions and see if there is sufficient triangulation between different data sources, and helps inform the design of questionnaires, interview schedules, and data tools, to ensure they support the gathering of necessary data (Better Evaluation, 2022). Therefore, the more ticks each area of the SIA gets, the more confidence that the data is providing an accurate picture.

Table 14 Triangulation matrix

	In-Depth Interviews	Survey	Observation	Technical Study	Academic Research
Baseline conditions		✓	✓		✓
Community aspirations	✓				
Opportunities	✓	✓	✓		
Vulnerabilities	✓	✓	✓		✓
Potential social impacts	✓	✓		✓	✓
Management strategies	✓			✓	✓
Enhancement strategies	✓			✓	✓

For further guidance on Triangulation visit Better Evaluation https://www.betterevaluation.org/methods-approaches/methods/triangulation

A Practical Guide to Social Impact Assessment

 ## 4.2.4 Stage 4 Social Impact Identification

You will need to review the data and information you collected to identify how the activities of the proposed project will create change for the baseline social conditions across the lifecycle. Therefore, you will need to use evidence from a range of data sources to enable you to identify the social impacts that require assessment as outlined in Table 15.

Table 15 Sources of evidence for social impact identification

Source	
Baseline	• Existing social conditions i.e., prior to the project e.g., health conditions, unemployment, cost of living, availability of housing and accommodation, weekly rents etc. • Vulnerable groups and people and their capacity. • Vulnerable locations, infrastructure and services.
Project design and activities	• Design elements that may have an impact on landholders, adjacent and nearby residents. • Activities that may have an impact on landholders, adjacent and nearby residents e.g., truck movements, workers camps etc.
CSE activities	• Issues raised by directly impacted landholders, nearby residents, vulnerable groups, businesses, First Nations peoples. • Level and quality of consultation e.g., was consultation comprehensive and transparent. • Information provided to community e.g., was it sufficient to empower them to participate meaningfully in the process.

SIA field study	• Impact, benefits and issues identified by participants. • Experiences of potentially affected landowners, residents etc.
Technical findings	• Breaches of standards and/or commonly accepted levels e.g., noise, air quality, water quality etc. • Environmental factors that have potential flow on effects for people e.g., increase traffic, influx of construction workforces.
Previous SIA's	• Effective social impact management and enhancement strategies. • Social impact and benefits that may be relevant or likely to occur as a consequence of the project.
Social research	• Evidence in academic and grey literature that supports the assessment.
Professional judgement	• Your social science knowledge and experience in social impact as well as human behaviour, social systems, and services, culture and social research.

Remember, when determining potential impacts look for how the project design and activities are likely to change or affect current social conditions for those residing and or doing business in the SIA study area.

4.2.5 Stage 5 Social Impact and Benefit Assessment

Now you have a comprehensive list of social impacts you need to assess each of them.

4.2.5.1 Step 1 Prepare for the assessment

Conducting a social risk workshop can help to ensure your assessment is well balanced and robust as you will be able to test the assumptions from multiple perspectives. This means you need to determine who will participate in the assessment of each of the identified impacts. A guide on who participates and their role in the social risk workshop is provided in Table 16.

Having the Client Project/Approvals Manager in attendance is preferred as it provides the client with a deep understanding of the assessment, improves robustness of residual impacts as the mitigation measures used during assessment will likely be agreed by the client, and no surprises to client when they receive the draft report and therefore improves the review process.

If they are unable or prefer not to participate, provide them with a brief that outlines the findings from the impact-benefit risk workshop for review and input.

Table 16 Participation guide for social risk workshop

Participants	Role
SIA Lead	Facilitate workshop
	Ensure all identified social impacts and benefits are rated
	Ensure data and evidence base support assessment
	Ensure all potential impacts and benefits consider appropriate management and enhancement measures
SIA delivery team	Participate in ensuring all identified social impacts and benefits raised during delivery of SIA are assessed
	Participate in providing the data and evidence base collected during delivery of the SIA
	Understanding of potential mitigation measures
Associate or above level Social Scientist not involved in SIA delivery	Provide objective technical input
	Actively provide checks and test assumptions
	Ensure robust assessment process
Preferred but optional participants:	
EIS Project Manager (if SIA is part of EIS process)	Provide detail understanding of the project
	Provide checks and test project specific assumptions
Client Project / Approval Manager	Provide detail understanding of the project
	Provide checks and test project specific assumptions

Communications deliver team member	Provide check and balance between SIA field study against issues raised by community during EIS engagement process

Before the workshop you should have all the inputs shown in Table 15. If one or more of the technical studies are not available, you will need to liaise with Project Manager and technical lead to determine when the outstanding studies to ascertain when the findings will be available.

Use a check list of all the inputs you need i.e., baseline study, research, field study findings, technical study findings, project description and list of identified social impacts.

If there are delays with one or more of the technical studies and timeframes are tight, the SIA Lead can negotiate with the EIS Project Manager to determine a way forward that does not jeopardise the assessment of social impacts or the delivery of the EIS.

Consider the timeframe and how you may manage the impact-benefit risk workshop if a technical study is unavailable e.g., can you proceed and incorporate findings once received, or do you need to reschedule the workshop?

Once all inputs are received send out invitations to participants and lock a time in their diary so you can convene a social risk workshop. Be sure to send all participants the relevant materials required to inform the assessment three days prior to the social risk workshop such as:

- Agenda (allocate time for each identified social impact).

- Full list of identified social impacts for assessment.

- Project description and relevant documentation, including activities across the lifecycle of the project.

- Relevant data and information related to the identified social impacts from:

    - Social baseline study

    - Research including academic and grey literature

    - Field study findings

    - Technical study findings

- Mitigation and Enhancement Strategies

- Commitments made by Proponent made to measure results and report findings

- Cumulative impacts (Section 3.2.7)

- Appropriate benchmarks

- Risk matrix and definitions to be used for determining the risk level.

4.2.5.2 Step 2 Conduct the social risk workshop

You will need to assess significance of the risk as a consequence of the project i.e., does the project change the existing social conditions. Each identified social impact needs to be assessed for the:

- Unmitigated or unenhanced risk i.e., the level of risk of the social impact occurring without the application of any mitigations or enhancement strategies, and

- Residual risk i.e. the level of risk once the mitigation and enhancement strategies are applied.

For each identified social impact follow the steps outlined below.

Step 2.1 Rating of likelihood

Use the definitions in Table 17 along with the relevant data and information to determine if the identified social impact is likely to occur as a consequence of the project activities (noting at what stage of the lifecycle e.g., construction, operation) without any mitigation or enhancement strategies adopted.

Once you have the unmitigated risk you then need to apply the mitigation and enhancement strategies and determine if their successful applications change the likelihood of the social impact occurring.

4 Conducting a Social impact Assessment

Table 17 Likelihood definitions of social impact

Highly likely	Has occurred in the past in this project (or operation) or in similar project OR circumstances could cause it to happen during the project (or operation).
Likely	Has occurred in the life of this project (or similar project) or in the last few years of operations or circumstances could cause it to occur again in the short term.
Possible	Has occurred at least once in this project or a similar project (or in the history of this operation).
Unlikely	Has never occurred in this project (or operation) but has occurred at other similar projects (operations) with similar risk/benefit profile.
Rare	Is possible but has not occurred to date in this project or similar projects.

Source: Adapted from State of New South Wales, 2023b

Use a spreadsheet that tracks your assessment of each of the identified impacts, i.e., their likelihood, dimensions and level of magnitude, significance rating along with the rationale for decision.

Step 2.2 Assess the magnitude

Now you have the likelihood, you now need to determine the magnitude of the unmitigated and residual risk for each identified social impact. Use the guiding questions for each of the dimensions of magnitude in Table 18. This will help you to understand who is impacted, for how long, how severely, how intensely and the level of interest or concern that exists.

Table 18 Dimensions of social impact magnitude

Dimensions	Questions to guide assessment
Extent	• Who specifically is expected to be affected (directly, indirectly, and/or cumulatively), including any vulnerable people? • Which location(s) and people are affected? (e.g. near neighbours, local, regional, future generations) • What external resources would be needed to recover from the impact? What would be the extent of the residual impact?
Duration	• When is the social impact expected to occur? • Will it be time-limited (e.g. over project phases) or permanent? • Will benefits be realised in the short-term, median-term or long-term?
Severity or scale	• What is the likely scale or degree of change? (e.g. mild, moderate, severe) • Are impacts going to be experienced immediately or gradually over time?
Intensity or importance	• How sensitive/vulnerable (or how adaptable/resilient) are affected people to the impact, or (for positive impacts) how important is it to them? This might depend on the value they attach to the matter; whether it is rare/unique or replaceable; the extent to which it is tied to their identity; and their capacity to cope with or adapt to change.

Level of concern / interest	• How concerned/interested are people? Sometimes, concerns may be disproportionate to findings from technical assessments of likelihood, duration and/or intensity? • What has the engagement with the community been like thus far? Has there been contention amongst the community?

Source: (State of New South Wales, 2023b)

Once you have identified the dimensions you will need to determine the level of the magnitude based on the definitions provided in Table 19.

Table 19 Definition of magnitude for social impact

Magnitude level	Definition
Transformational	Substantial change experienced in community wellbeing, livelihood, infrastructure, services, health, and/or heritage values; permanent displacement or addition of at least 20% of a community.
Major	Substantial deterioration/improvement to something that people value highly, either lasting for an indefinite time, or affecting many people in a widespread area.
Moderate	Noticeable deterioration/improvement to something that people value highly, either lasting for an extensive time, or affecting a group of people.

Minor	Mild deterioration/improvement for a reasonably short time, for a small number of people who are generally adaptable and not vulnerable.
Minimal	Little noticeable change experienced by people in the study area.

Source: (State of New South Wales, 2023b)

Step 2.2 Assess the magnitude

Now you should have for each identified social impact:

- Unmitigated / unenhanced risk: likelihood (highly likely, likely, possible, unlikely or rare) and magnitude level (transformational, major, moderate, minor, minimal).

- Residual risk: likelihood (highly likely, likely, possible, unlikely or rare) and magnitude level (transformational, major, moderate, minor, minimal).

These will have been informed by the data and information. Now you will use the social impact significance matrix (Table 20) to determine the significance of each of the social impacts (both unmitigated/unenhanced and residual). For example:

Likely + Moderate Magnitude = High Significance

4 Conducting a Social impact Assessment

Table 20 Social impact significance matrix

Likelihood level	Magnitude level				
	Minimal	Minor	Moderate	Major	Transformational
Almost certain	Low	Medium	High	Very High	Very High
Likely	Low	Medium	High	High	Very High
Possible	Low	Medium	Medium	High	High
Unlikely	Low	Low	Medium	Medium	High
Very Unlikely	Low	Low	Low	Medium	Medium

Source: (State of New South Wales, 2023b)

These tables will help inform the likely significance of each impact before mitigation/enhancement. However, these tables may also be re-applied to assess residual social impacts or benefits and thereby demonstrate the effectiveness of proposed mitigation/enhancement measures.

 ### 4.2.6 Stage 6 Social Impact Management Plan

The social impact management plan will include:

❖ A project summary.

❖ How engagement with community members i.e., field study activities (Section 3.2.2), project and EIS CSE activities (Section 1.9).

- All identified social impacts (Section 3.2.4 and their social risk ranking (unmitigated/unenhanced and residual) as identified in Section 3.2.5.

- Identified mitigation and enhancement strategies applied in the social risk workshop to help determine the residual risk (Section 3.2.5.2).

- Commitment by client e.g., measurement of results and reporting the findings via the project website (State of New South Wales, 2023a).

- Activities, outputs, outcomes and metrics for measurement for each all mitigation and enhancement strategies.

- Monitoring and management strategy that outlines the auditing and reviewing process including timing, frequency, method and responsibilities.

- Commitment to delivery of the SIMP and reporting of results and findings, including how shortfall will be addressed, on the project website.

4.2.6.1 Mitigation and Enhancement Strategies

The SIA should provide management measures for all potentially significant negative impacts and must demonstrate that the hierarchy of avoid and mitigate (Section 1.3) has been followed. This would require that reasonable measures have been undertaken to avoid the negative social impacts i.e., measures related to project design, location, consultation and implementation before proposing mitigation measures (Government - Office of the Coordinator-General, 2018). An SIA should also consider enhancement strategies for positive impacts to ensure the maximisation and monitoring of potential benefits. The SIMP should incorporate capacity building strategies that are aimed at ensuring vulnerable individuals and groups are able to participate and adapt to changes.

4.2.6.2 Monitoring and Evaluation

The purpose of monitoring is to:

- Track the progress and assess the appropriateness and effectiveness of the management measures.

- Assess the actual project impacts against the potential impacts and social indicators identified in the SIA.

> Consider adopting an adaptive management approach. Applying a structured process for making decisions in the face of uncertainty, with the goal of reducing uncertainty over time will allow for adjustment to mitigation strategies as new information arises.

- Capture information with which to advise potentially impacted communities and government on progress and achievements.

- Facilitate engagement, consultation and collaboration with stakeholders (Government - Office of the Coordinator-General, 2018).

The key components of a monitoring program are:

❖ A list of identified impacts, issues and benefits

❖ Targets and outcomes sought

❖ Description of how management measures will be monitored and reported.

❖ The party responsible for monitoring

❖ Timing and frequency of monitoring

❖ Key performance indicators

❖ Mechanisms to update management measures as required (Government - Office of the Coordinator-General, 2018).

Setting specific, measurable, achievable, relevant, and time-bound (SMART) objectives is a good way to plan the steps to meet the long-term goals in your SIMP.

4.2.7 Stage 7 Cumulative Impacts

Consideration should be given to potential cumulative impacts that could result from the combined effect of similar actions by multiple projects. Although cumulative impacts may not be within the proponent's direct control, an assessment provides important context regarding the likely consequences that would be experienced by potentially impacted communities (Government - Office of the Coordinator-General, 2018).

An example of consequences from multiple projects that overlap is how the community may experience a worsened impacts from construction e.g., dust and noise or multiple projects needing similar resources (skilled labour, housing or water). The most effective way to assess cumulative social impacts is to consider them from the viewpoint of those experiencing them (State of New South Wales, 2023a).To conduct this assessment, you will need a list of all proposed project in the regional that overlap the timeframe of your project, including the following information:

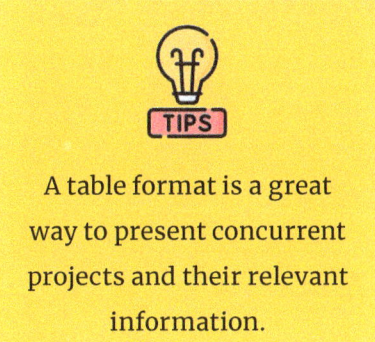

A table format is a great way to present concurrent projects and their relevant information.

❖ Anticipated length of time of the project

❖ Development type e.g., mining, waste, solar farm, wind farm

- Status of the project i.e., operational, preparing EIS, assessment, approved

- Determination date

- Construction workforce numbers

- Current or expected operational workforce numbers (full time equivalent).

Once you have the information assess the effect of combined incremental and cumulative impacts on people by considering them from the points of view of the people who are likely to experience them.

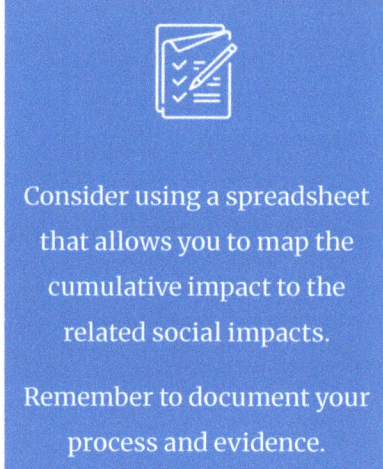

Consider using a spreadsheet that allows you to map the cumulative impact to the related social impacts.

Remember to document your process and evidence.

4.2.7.1 Step 1 Determine cumulative impacts

Now you have the list of overlapping projects, are there any that change the nature or intensity the identified social impacts (Section 3.2.4). The cumulative impacts can be categorised as:

- Spatial impacts: occur over the same time e.g., construction activities of multiple projects that produce cumulative noise and air quality impacts commonly experiences along haulage routes.

❖ Temporal impacts: vary over time e.g., construction of multiple large projects over the same time period may require temporary workers in the same are that may create a cumulative shortage of housing and accommodation.

❖ Linked impacts: complex interactions where one impact may trigger another, or a single activity may have multiple impacts. For example, a project may generate noise and dust, consume local water resources or increase traffic on local roads.

4.2.7.2 Step 2 Assess cumulative effects

For each of the identified cumulative impacts apply the response in Table 21 for each cumulative impact.

Table 21 Responses to assess cumulative effects

Yes	Existence of combined or cumulative impacts which affect people in these ways
No	This social impact is isolated from cumulative impacts
Unknown	Unclear whether there will be cumulative impacts that affect people
N/A	This social impact is not relevant to the project

Source: (State of New South Wales, 2023c)

Specify which social impacts produce cumulative impacts when considering all those that get a response 'Yes' or 'Unknown' (State of New South Wales, 2023c).

4.2.8 Stage 8 Reporting

Now you have completed your assessment you will present your method and findings in an SIA Report. Some projects may not require a standalone report and instead a Social Impact Chapter (or Social Chapter) that sits within the EIS Report. I will provide an outline for both.

4.2.8.1 Standalone SIA Report

If you are preparing a standalone SIA you will need to include information that would not be required of you in an SIA Chapter e.g., project description and an executive summary. Below is an SIA Report outline:

Executive Summary
1. Introduction
    1.1. Overview
    1.2. Assessment approach and requirements
2. Project description
    2.1. The site
    2.2. Project description
    2.3. Project transport
3. Methodology
    3.4. Area of social influence
    3.5. Potentially affected communities
    3.6. Methodological approach
4. Political and planning context
    4.1. Federal
    4.2. State
    4.3. Local

4 Conducting a Social impact Assessment

1. Social baseline
    1.1. Area of social influence
    1.2. Demographics
    1.3. Qualifications and workforce
    1.4. Local business and industry
    1.5. Social infrastructure and services
    1.6. Housing and accommodation
    1.7. Health and wellbeing
    1.8. Vulnerable groups and vulnerabilities
2. Community and stakeholder engagement
    2.1. Project CSE
    2.2. EIS engagement activities and participation
    2.3. SIA field study activities
3. Social impact assessment
4. Mitigation and management
    6.1. Monitoring and management framework
5. Acronyms
6. References
7. Appendix: Social Baseline Study

Below are links to examples of SIA Reports:

- New Cobar Complex:
  https://www.planningportal.nsw.gov.au/major-projects/projects/new-cobar-complex-project
- Gunlake Quarry Continuation Project:
  https://www.planningportal.nsw.gov.au/major-projects/projects/gunlake-quarry-continuation-project
- Snowy 2.0 Segment Factory:
  https://www.planningportal.nsw.gov.au/major-projects/projects/snowy-20-segment-factory

❖ New Primary School at Edmondson Park: https://www.planningportal.nsw.gov.au/major-projects/projects/new-primary-school-edmondson-park

4.2.8.2 Social Chapter

If you are preparing an SIA Chapter, the level of detail will depend on the scale of the SIA. An example of the SIA Chapter outline is below:

1. Overview
2. Existing environment (this is your social baseline)
   2.1. Study area / area of social influence
   2.2. Relevant social planning context
   2.3. Demographic profile
   2.4. Vulnerable people and places
3. Potential impact
4. Mitigation and management
5. Acronyms
6. References

TIPS

Your Chapter will form part of the EIS Report so make sure to communicate with the EIS Project Manager (PM) before you commence writing. Find out the requirements for format and style.

 ### 4.2.9 Stage 9 Submissions

The submissions phase will require you to respond to agency and feedback from public consultation or exhibition activities. These responses often have regulatory timeframes attached. You will need to go the agency responsible for the

4 Conducting a Social impact Assessment

regulatory process or speak to the EIS project manager, so you know what is expected.

To assist in providing adequate and timely responses you will need to:

❖ Document your process for all stages of the SIA.

❖ Be able to articulate the evidence base that supports your assessment.

❖ Demonstrate you have met the statutory and regulatory requirements.

TIPS

Filing is important for being able to go back and access information. Remember version control and clear documentation is important e.g., checklists, attendee lists, distribution lists, dates of field study activities etc.

Keep a spreadsheet that outlines how you assessed each social impact and supporting evidence.

5 List of Resources and Regulation

Resource	Link
IAIA Resources	https://www.iaia.org/resources.php
IFC Performance Standards on Environmental and Social Sustainability	https://www.ifc.org/en/insights-reports/2012/ifc-performance-standards
World Bank Environmental and Social Framework	https://www.worldbank.org/en/projects-operations/environmental-and-social-framework
United Nations (UN) Sustainable Development Goals	https://sdgs.un.org/goals
World Health Organisation (WHO) Social Determinants of Health	https://www.who.int/health-topics/social-determinants-of-health#tab=tab_1
WHO Health and Wellbeing	https://www.who.int/Data/Gho/Data/Major-Themes/Health-and-Well-Being
Social Capital Research	https://www.socialcapitalresearch.com/
	https://www.oecd.org/en/publications/four-interpretations-of-social-capital_5jzbcx010wmt-en.html
OECD Measuring Social Connectedness	https://www.oecd.org/en/publications.html

ABS Measuring Social Capital	https://www.ausstats.abs.gov.au/ausstats/free.nsf/0/13C0688F6B98DD45CA256E360077D526/$File/13780_2004.pdf
World Bank Gini Index (Poverty and Inequity)	https://data.worldbank.org/indicator/SI.POV.GINI
OECD Better Life Index	https://www.oecdbetterlifeindex.org/
Global Wellness Institute Happiness and Wellbeing Indices	https://globalwellnessinstitute.org/industry-research/%20happiness-wellbeing-index/
Australian Government Measuring What Matters	https://treasury.gov.au/policy-topics/measuring-what-matters
Social Value International Standards and Guidance	https://www.socialvalueint.org/standards-and-guidance
International Association for Public Participation	https://iap2.org.au/resources/
Institute for Human Rights	https://www.ihrb.org/resources
UN Consultation and free, prior and informed consent	https://www.ohchr.org/en/topic/indigenous-peoples
International Council on Mining and Metals, Social Performance	https://www.icmm.com/en-gb/guidance/social-performance/2022/tools-for-social-performance

International Hydropower Association	https://www.hydropower.org/
Australasian Institute of Mining and Metallurgy	https://www.ausimm.com/insights-and-resources/
Australasian Centre for Corporate Responsibility	https://www.accr.org.au/
Regulatory Frameworks	
African Development Bank Group	https://www.afdb.org/sites/default/files/documents/environmental-and-social-assessments/esmf-rss-final_main.en-final.pdf
Asian Development Bank Environmental (ADB) and Social Framework	https://www.adb.org/publications
ADB Environmental and Social Requirements	https://www.adb.org/publications
Arab Petroleum Corporation	https://www.apicorp.org/wp-content/uploads/2022/02/APICORP_ESG_Policy_Framework_v5.0.pdf
European Investment Bank	https://www.eib.org/en/publications/environmental-and-social-standards-2018
Inter-American Development Bank	https://www.iadb.org/en/who-we-are/topics/environmental-and-social-solutions/environmental-and-social-policy-framework

United States National Environmental Policy Act (NEPA), 1969 Policies and Guidance	https://www.epa.gov/nepa/national-environmental-policy-act-policies-and-guidance
United Kingdom	https://www.gov.uk

6 Acronyms

Acronym	In Full
ABS	Australian Bureau of Statistics
ADB	Asian Development Bank
AI	Artificial intelligence
AIHW	Australian Institute of Health and Wellbeing
BIBO	bus-in bus out
CATI	Computer Assisted Telephone Interviewing
CSE	Community and stakeholder engagement
COPD	chronic obstructive pulmonary disease
CV	Curriculum Vitai
DIDO	drive-in drive out
DPE	Department of Planning and Environment
EIS	Environmental Impact Statement
e.g.	For example
EP&A Act	Environmental Planning & Assessment Act 1979
ESIA	Environmental and social impact statement
Etc	Etcetera
FGD	Focus group discussion
FIFO	Fly-in fly out
FPIC	Free, prior, and informed consent
FTE	Full time equivalent
GIS	geographic information system
HSE	Health, Safety and Environment
IFC	International Finance Corporation
IAIA	International Association for Impact Assessment
IAP2	International Association for Public Participation
ICSEA	Index of Community Socio-Educational Advantage

JSA	Journey safety assessment
Km	Kilometre
LGA	Local government area
Ltd	Limited
m	Metre
Mw	Megawatt
MWH	Megawatt per hour
NAPLAN	National Assessment Program—Literacy and Numeracy
n.d.	No date
NSW	New South Wales
OECD	Organisation for Economic Co-operation and Development
OCG	Office of Coordinator General
Pty	Proprietary
PPE	Personal protection equipment
RFP	Request for proposal
RFI	Request for information
UN	United Nations
SA2	Suburb
SDG	Sustainable Development Goals
SEIFA	Socio-economic indexes for Areas
SIA	Social impact assessment
SIMP	Social impact management plan
SPSS	Statistical Package for Social Sciences
SSD	State Significant Development
SSRC Act	Strong and Sustainable Resource Communities Act
UK	United Kingdom
WHO	World Health Organisation

7 References

Australian Bureau of Statistics. (n.d.). *Quantitative and qualitative data.* Retrieved November 25, 2024, from https://www.abs.gov.au/statistics/understanding-statistics/statistical-terms-and-concepts/quantitative-and-qualitative-data

Australian Government. (1992). *Intergovernmental Agreement on the Environment.*

Australian Institute of Aboriginal and Torres Strait Islander Studies. (n.d.). *Engaging with Traditional Owners.* Retrieved February 5, 2025, from https://nativetitle.org.au/find/pbc

Better Evaluation. (2022). *Triangulation.* https://www.betterevaluation.org/methods-approaches/methods/triangulation

Bingham, A. J. (2023). From Data Management to Actionable Findings: A Five-Phase Process of Qualitative Data Analysis. *International Journal of Qualitative Methods, 22.* https://doi.org/10.1177/16094069231183620/ASSET/IMAGES/LARGE/10.1177_16094069231183620-FIG11.JPEG

Coakes, S., & Anagnostaras, J. (2024). *29. Social research methods for project social impact assessment.* https://www.elgaronline.com/

Corrs Chambers Westgarth. (2023, May 1). *FPIC in the Australian context: now and into the future.* https://www.corrs.com.au/insights/fpic-in-the-australian-context-now-and-into-the-future#

Food and Agriculture Organization. (2016). *Free Prior and Informed Consent: An indigenous peoples' right and a good practice for local communities.* https://openknowledge.fao.org/server/api/core/bitstreams/8a4bc655-3cf6-44b5-b6bb-ad2aeede5863/content

Government - Office of the Coordinator-General, Q. (2018). *Social Impact Assessment (SIA) Guideline - March 2018.* www.statedevelopment.qld.gov.au/cg

International Association for Public Participation. (2018). *IAP2 Spectrum of Public Participation.*

International Finance Corporation. (2012). *IFC Performance Standards on Environmental and Social Sustainability.*

Kulik, R. M. (2024). Social issue. In *Encyclopedia Britannica.* https://www.britannica.com/topic/social-issue

Mizrak, F. (2023). Driving Social and Environmental Impact: Exploring Sustainability and Corporate Social Responsibility Frameworks. In *Innovation, Strategy, and Transformation Frameworks for the Modern Enterprise* (p. 19). https://doi.org/10.4018/979-8-3693-0458-7.ch015

7 References

Palinkas, L. A., Horwitz, S. M., Green, C. A., Wisdom, J. P., Duan, N., & Hoagwood, K. (2015). Purposeful sampling for qualitative data collection and analysis in mixed method implementation research. *Administration and Policy in Mental Health*, 42(5), 533. https://doi.org/10.1007/S10488-013-0528-Y

Sopact. (n.d.). *Social Impact Guide*. Retrieved February 5, 2025, from https://www.sopact.com/guides/social-impact#

State of New South Wales. (2023a). *Social Impact Assessment Guideline for State Significant Projects*. www.dpie.nsw..ov.au

State of New South Wales. (2023b). *Technical Supplement: Social Impact Assessment Guideline for State Significant Projects*. www.planning.nsw.gov.au/sia

State of New South Wales. (2023c). *Technical Supplement: Social Impact Assessment Guideline for State Significant Projects*. www.planning.nsw.gov.au/sia

United States Environmental Protection Agency. (2025). *Cumulative Impacts Research*. https://www.epa.gov/healthresearch/cumulative-impacts-research#

Vanclay, F. (2003). *SIA principles International Principles For Social Impact Assessment* (Vol. 21, Issue 1). Beech Tree Publishing. www.iaia.org

www.ingramcontent.com/pod-product-compliance
Lightning Source LLC
Chambersburg PA
CBHW061221070526
44584CB00029B/3931